STEAM BENEATH THE RED STAR

STEAM
BENEATH THE
RED STAR

Previous page: An L class Soviet Railways Decapod steamed through scenic Russian forestland. —Ian Button

By Ron Ziel and Nils Huxtable

AMEREON HOUSE
Mattituck, New York U.S.A.

SUNRISE SPECIAL LTD.
Bridgehampton, New York U.S.A

STEAMSCENES
West Vancouver, B.C., Canada

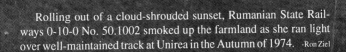

Rolling out of a cloud-shrouded sunset, Rumanian State Railways 0-10-0 No. 50.1002 smoked up the farmland as she ran light over well-maintained track at Unirea in the Autumn of 1974. -Ron Ziel

DEDICATION

To the many railway officials, workers and transport police, as well as other security personnel, military officers and ordinary citizens who, often at their own personal risk, assisted the authors and contributors in the countries behind the Iron Curtain, this book is gratefully dedicated.

Other Books Written by the Authors

NILS HUXTABLE

DAYLIGHT REFLECTIONS

CLASSIC NORTH AMERICAN STEAM

CLASSIC STEAM LOCOMOTIVES OF THE WORLD

BRITISH STEAM REVIVAL (with Pete Skelton)

STEAM SPIRIT (with Tom Schultz)

NARROW GAUGE...THEN AND NOW (with Tom Gildersleeve)

RON ZIEL

THE TWILIGHT OF STEAM LOCOMOTIVES

THE STORY OF STEAMTOWN AND EDAVILLE

STEEL RAILS TO THE SUNRISE (with George H. Foster)

STEAM IN THE SIXTIES (with George H. Foster)

STEEL RAILS TO VICTORY

SOUTHERN STEAM SPECIALS (with Mike Eagleson)

THE TWILIGHT OF WORLD STEAM (with Mike Eagleson)

LONG ISLAND HERITAGE, THE G-5

THE PENNSY ERA ON LONG ISLAND

ELECTRIC HERITAGE OF THE L.I.R.R. (with John Krause)

VICTORIAN RAILROAD STATIONS OF LONG ISLAND (with Richard B. Wettereau)

THE L.I.R.R. IN EARLY PHOTOGRAPHS

MAINLINE STEAM REVIVAL

AMERICAN LOCOMOTIVES IN HISTORIC PHOTOGRAPHS

ACKNOWLEDGEMENTS

The authors are indebted to many individuals, government ministries and officials, as well as railway personnel, for their assistance in obtaining photographs and information concerning steam locomotives on the railways of former and present-day Communist countries. First and foremost are the photographers who generously made their own work and collections available. Official cooperation was expedited by Mrs. Stefania Dabkowska of the Polish Ministry of Commmunication, by the Chinese Railways and, eventually and reluctantly, by the Yugoslav Railways. Special mention must be given to Florian Schmidt, who supplied detailed railroad histories of North Korea and Vietnam, and Ian D. Johnson, who made additional DPRK material available, as did Sylvia Estandarte-Breva. Vera Paclewsky and Vincent F. Seyfried translated Russian articles and Ladislava Štěpánová helped with Czech place names. Wayne Weiss was a valuable source of Cuban railway knowledge. Tim Murray provided lodging for the authors in London. In addition to writing the Introduction and contributing much of the earliest and rarest photographic work, A.E. Durrant also housed and advised the authors. Rüdiger Weber, Ed Miller, Thomas R. Schultz, Margaret Matthews-Ziel, George Bambery, Robert Kingsford-Smith, David Moulden, David Needham, Mike Tyack and Ian Simpson shared the discomforts of primitive travel arrangements. Robert Koch helped considerably with the China chapter. Thanks are also due to Valentin Pashkevitch and the Dzherelo staff, as well as Reggie Tonry of World Rail Travel Specialists for making the authors' Ukrainian steam tour so successful. Bill Alborough of TEFS and Lance King of the Continental Railway Circle publicized the authors' efforts and provided assistance. Typesetting was done by Kristin Von Eiff of Reflective Image, Mattituck, New York. Finally, Ian Button furnished historical Soviet Railways photos and information.

AUTHORS' NOTE: Many of the photographs of the steam locomotives of Communist railway systems used in this book, plus thousands more, in color and black-and-white, are available to private collectors, institutions, museums and libraries. Inquiries, including those regarding publication and advertising use, should be addressed to: Sunrise Special Ltd., Box 433, Bridgehampton, New York, 11932, USA. Telephone: (516) 726-9544.

Art direction, design, and paste-up work by Ron Ziel.

Manufactured in the United States of America.

International Standard Book Number 0-8488-0929-7

TABLE OF CONTENTS

INTRODUCTION..........6

FOREWORD 8

SOVIET UNION 14

HUNGARY...............36

POLAND 50

EAST GERMANY 74

CZECHOSLOVAKIA 96

YUGOSLAVIA 126

ALBANIA 153

BULGARIA.............154

RUMANIA 168

NORTH KOREA 192

VIETNAM 196

CHINA 204

CUBA 230

BIBLIOGRAPHY 256

Chinese QJ 2-10-2s Nos. 2497 and 6999 worked an oil train above a frozen river between Zhongwei and Gantang on January 20, 1992.

Pete Skelton

INTRODUCTION

Steam Beneath The Red Star existed since Russia's Bolshevik Revolution, more than three-quarters of a century ago, beyond the ken of most people today, and for thirty years was limited to that unfortunate country. From the end of World War II, well within living memory, the Soviets extended their iron grip over much of Eastern Europe, and many of the world's most fascinating steam locomotives suddenly were hidden behind the "Iron Curtain". The paranoid security *apparat* of formerly free countries, euphemistically designated "peoples' democracies", made the photography of railways a forbidden pastime for those few allowed in, while most foreigners were not even permitted entry to the communistic domains. Outside of the Soviet Russian bloc, this harsh regime was found in China and several neighboring countries in Asia, as well as Cuba.

Within the above background the placid and often bumbling railway enthusiast was clearly out of place, but in most cases, such were content with the trains in their homelands. However, within the ranks of the predominantly parochial railfan community, there was a handful to whom the local lines (especially after dieselisation) were passé – dare one say boring – and like the adventurers of old, were attracted to the challenge of the call of far whistles, the roar of distant exhausts and the clanking of rods within societies where a dissident word meant instant repression.

The authors and this writer are among that small, strange community of international steam enthusiasts willing to endure anything for the master shot of an exotic locomotive, purloined under the watchful glare of the hostile guardians of an alien environment. The satisfaction thus derived was exquisite – the knowledge of getting something which few others, perhaps nobody else in the world possessed. Of course, we of that fraternity are often considered mad, but why not be – in today's world of homogenous conformity, so-called "sane" people indulging in "normal" pursuits can be so terribly *boring*.

Towards the end of my Army servitude came the news that Yugoslavia's Marshal Tito had broken with the Moscow mob and that tourism from the West was to be encouraged, even to the extent of half-price rail tickets for those with tourist visas! A recording of Bloch's *Schelomo* encouraged the distant call of the Orient and my demobilisation leave was spent, in late 1952, in a tentative exploration of Yugoslavia's remarkable stock of oft outlandish steam locomotives. My introduction to the red star countries was dramatic, if not somewhat tedious. Crossing from Italy's Poggiarale Campagna border station to Sežana, Yugoslavia, set in the appropriately harsh *Karst* country, the train was surrounded by grey-uniformed police with red star cap badges, whilst the yard was full of grey-painted wagons bearing the inscriptien JDZ-J in Roman and Cyrillic lettering. The police were very thorough and suspicious, investigating inside and outside the train, including underneath. It was, I suppose, a very good introduction to a Communist regime – everything very grey and all authority extremely suspicious.

Bulgaria alone, before 1958, issued transit visas for passage to and from Istanbul on the *Orient Express*, on such few through coaches as made the journey. Stopovers within Bulgaria were forbidden, but on the two occasions that I made this trip, the train from Turkey lost so much time, that all connections were missed, leading to daylight transit through Bulgaria: very frustrating, since my camera equipment had been sealed! These and many more were typical of the adventures encountered in the pursuit of Eastern European steam locomotives, but the fascination of the "prey" was so great that the discomforts of one trip were soon forgotten – especially after the film was processed – and plans made to repeat what had been unsuccessfully covered, or to explore further what looked like interesting leads. In all of these visits, no form of official permission to photograph was ever obtained, and even to request such a thing only served to arouse suspicion. In 1953, whilst still employed in the drawing office of British Railways' Locomotive Works at Swindon, I applied for visitor visas, honestly stating my reasons as a railwayman interested in seeing the railway installations of the various countries concerned. Despite several requests for clarification, my visa applications were ignored (They were not even refused.) Yet, my requests for free passes through the several countries, processed via railway channels, were all granted, and I found myself in the situation of having free railway passes in countries I was unable to enter due to lack of visas! Such were the results of the paranoid suspicions and bungling bureacracies in the Communist system!

Within afew years after the death of Stalin, in 1953, the iron glove was to ease its grip and Eastern European countries allowed tourists in, simply for the sake of the hard currency they would spend. Originally, one had to plan a rigid programme, with hotels booked and paid for in advance, limiting any flexibility which local conditions suggested, but as everywhere was unexplored and information as to where the more interesting locomotives were te be found was discovered purely by trial and error, one guess as to where to go was as good as another. On all of my visits East I was alone, there being few wishing to see these fascinating railway systems – and fewer willing to take the risks involved. Perhaps this was fortunate, a single person being less obtrusive than a group chattering in a foreign language, and alone I succeeded where several may have failed.

In retrospect, it was all very worthwhile. I was scared to death in Rumania (by far the most paranoid state) when the secret police interrogating me suggested that

One of "Dusty" Durrant's memorable early red star photographs: Hungarian-built 4-8-0s Nos. 11.059 and 11.062 doubleheaded the main daytime express from Split to Zagreb through barren scenery at Kastel Stari, Yugoslavia, on September 14, 1959. -A.E. Durrant

if I "disappeared" on a trip which included Czechoslovakia, Hungary and Bulgaria as well, nobody would know in which country I had been lost! Yet, there were the hilarious moments, such as the big booze-up in Bulgaria where everybody loved me, the women wanted British coins depicting the head of the Queen, a new bottle of local wine being broached almost for every penny produced, whilst the scowling party spy viewing these goings-on with increasing disgust was eventually jeered off the premises!

Most of my photographs got home safely; a few rolls were surreptitiously stolen by the Bulgarian secret police, filched from my bag in the hotel while I was out photographing their glorious 2-12-4T locomotives. They were only missed when the tally of processed negatives failed to match my notes, and as one missing film was from that country, my case was proven, not that anything could be done about it! Then there was the roll of film developed in Yugoslavia on orders from the local police and returned to me dripping wet a few minutes before the departure of my train. As this included what were probably the first ever photographs of the Bulgarian 2-12-4Ts (the day before) to get out of the country, I was particularly anxious concerning their preservation, drying them in the breeze from the moving train, spending the next night in a hotel at Cacak, re-rinsing, drying and wrapping in rather coarse toilet paper, before getting them home to London. First thing was to have whole plate prints made, big enough to copy in case the film had been improperly fixed, but forty years later they remain in good order, having recently been satisfyingly printed for this book.

Then there were the explanations, during various interrogations, as to *why* one would take photographs of steam trains. Even in an open Western society, with numerous lunatic fringes, this is often difficult to explain and was even moreso to the brain-washed victims of Communist orthodoxy. A "hobby" was instantly dismissed – hobbies were only those rendered officially respectable, such as stamp collecting, playing chess or watching football. Admittedly, Western convention is equally scathing; those who fail to play golf or become teleholics, are similarly looked down upon by their alleged peers. My second trip to Czechoslovakia provided an acceptable answer used several times later with complete success. I was taking photographs for "a nephew who likes trains" and this bamboozled the locals sufficiently to release me and my film. Had they ever caught on to the fact that the whole trip was designed for steam photography, their own avuncular instincts would have been suspect forever!

Eastern Europe was the start of my writing career, commencing with a series of articles in a little magazine, *EUROPEAN RAILWAYS*, leading thence to my first book, *THE STEAM LOCOMOTIVES OF EASTERN EUROPE*. From there it was an easy series of steps to the rest of the world: Asia, Africa, Australasia and South America, but the old Eastern European steam remains as fascinating as ever. I have known both authors for years and have "photted" steam trains with them in various parts of the world, including South Africa and China. The chance to contribute towards *STEAM BENEATH THE RED STAR* has led to happy sessions in my darkroom, exhuming old negatives and producing better prints from them than were originally supplied by commercial agencies – or the secret police!

-A. E. Durrant , Springs, South Africa

FOREWORD

There could have been no better introduction to red star steam than in the city of Khabarovsk, in far eastern Siberia. Discolored by soot, grey snow lay on the roofs, in the streets and along the tracks of the Trans-Siberian Railway. Solidified, the snow would not melt for months. Only the old women in felt boots, padded coats and headscarves seemed to be making any progress in snow removal, chipping it away from the station platform where train No. 1, the westbound *Rossiya* ("Russia"), would soon be making its grand entrance behind a green and red-liveried P36 4-8-4.

In the early 1970s, with the possibility of a thaw in the Cold War as remote as a thaw in Siberia in January, the P36, like most everything else in the Soviet Union, was shrouded in mystery: "We knew they were there, but why and how long (and the style of their steaming) were unknown", according to the late David P. Morgan, the editor of *TRAINS* magazine. Writing of the first trip to track down the recondite P36 by one of the co-authors in the July, 1971 issue of his renowned periodical, Morgan concluded: "Now, thanks to this intrepid chronicler of steam regardless of its national colors, we are on speaking terms with the great multi-hued P36 Soviet

steam star." Originally, the roller-bearing Northerns from Kolomna – the last mainline steam-power to be built in the USSR – had been showpiece engines, working the trains most frequented by foreign visitors: Brest -Moscow and between the capital and such important centers as Leningrad; Lvov and the frontiers of Rumania and Poland, until the 4-8-4s were displaced by electrification. By the late 1960s, many were exiled to the Far East, beyond Irkutsk.

The *Rossiya* – prestige express on the Trans-Siberian – made the journey through eight time zones between Khabarovsk and Moscow in six days, by far the longest passenger train run in the world. The easternmost 2500 miles of the route – between Lake Baikal and the Pacific – saw Trains 1 and 2 still entrusted to relays of P36 4-8-4 power – one of the most beautiful classes of locomotive in existence – sometimes double-heading, with changes of engines and crews every 250 miles or so. As the *Proyekt 36* made its dignified appearance, one could only marvel at its sheer height - seventeen feet from railhead to skyline casing. The Boxpok driving wheels, ribbed smoke deflectors and "lightning flash" stripe from pilot to tender, enhanced the impression of power and beauty made on a first-time observer. Truly, this was the ultimate in red star steam! A furtive glance and the photographer yielded to temptation, withdrawing

Serbian 2-6-2 No. 01.094 left electrified trackage at Lapovo, Croatia, on a July, 1980 evening.   Ron Ziel

a camera from beneath his parka. A locomotive such as this was worth the risk!

In the 1970s, the Soviet Union, its satellites, plus Yugoslavia, China and Cuba, provided some of the most exciting steam shows anywhere. An incredible variety of locomotive types, old and new, attracted the photographer willing to lead a double life: that of innocent tourist and security-endangering "spy". In countries beneath the red star, railroad facilities and equipment were considered to be of strategic importance, immediately alerting the paranoid instincts of not only the police, but often ordinary citizens as well. Steam photographers harbored no illusions and were well-prepared long before leaving the free air of home, for the tourist information provided by each of the Communist regimes all contained a similar ominous admonition: "Photography of military installations, industrial sites, bridges, tunnels and railways is strictly forbidden." Indeed, in the 1970s, the United States Mission in Berlin handed a stern brochure to any of its citizens who inquired about traveling to East Berlin and "the Soviet Zone of Germany", which was not recognized by the U.S. government as anything more than an occupied military district. Several excerpts which did not exactly instill confidence in the authors and others who were assiduously pursuing the 2000 steamers of the *Deutsche Reichsbahn* with nothing but photography in mind: "The United States...is not in a position to extend to American

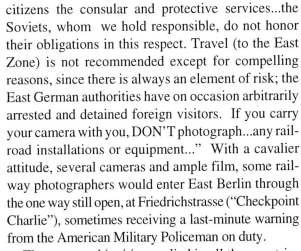

citizens the consular and protective services...the Soviets, whom we hold responsible, do not honor their obligations in this respect. Travel (to the East Zone) is not recommended except for compelling reasons, since there is always an element of risk; the East German authorities have on occasion arbitrarily arrested and detained foreign visitors. If you carry your camera with you, DON'T photograph...any railroad installations or equipment..." With a cavalier attitude, several cameras and ample film, some railway photographers would enter East Berlin through the one way still open, at Friedrichstrasse ("Checkpoint Charlie"), sometimes receiving a last-minute warning from the American Military Policeman on duty.

The same ambiguities applied in all the countries of what the Red propagandists referred to as "the Socialist Camp." Occasionally, railway photographers were welcomed; more likely they would be hauled into the local police station. Attitudes could shift virtually overnight – even in dour and ossified Communist republics. After being the most risky of countries for the railroad photographer, East Germany, in 1973, suddenly decided that such odd foreigners spent lots of dollars, francs, pounds and marks, and abruptly, many of the restrictions were lifted. Similarly, Rumania, which A. E. Durrant had declared to be "by far the most paranoid state" in the early 1960s, co-author Ziel (but not co-author Huxtable) found to be perhaps the most reasonable a decade later. In most cases, however, without a special permit (the coveted *Genehmigung* in East Germany), unobtainable except for organized groups and citizens of neutral countries (i.e. Austria), the individual photographer was looking for trouble. *It* often found *him*.

In all red star countries of Europe the hazards of steam photography were formidable, and only by spending fleeting interludes at the lineside could the cameraman hope to keep the film he had exposed. It was necessary to be wary of anyone, particularly a lower-ranking Party flunky or a police informer, who relished making a citizen's arrest and turning in a "Western spy". Even railwaymen could turn vigilante: the crew of a Hungarian 2-6-2 once stopped their local passenger train, leaped from the cab and demanded to see Ziel's non-existent photo permit, later alerting the police, who set up a road block and apprehended him. Two machinists at Molodechno shed, Byelorussia (now Belarus) turned Huxtable in to the local Party functionary; he informed the KGB. On one occasion, a Polish engine driver and fireman, after bringing their train to a halt, pursued an unfortu-

nate photographer into the woods, where they beat him with tree branches! When a scowling engineman leaned out of the cab and crossed his wrists (especially in Yugoslavia), the inference was clear: handcuffs awaited the enthusiast in the next town.

More typically, the culprit who had been spotted was apprehended, escorted to a "conference room" at the local police station and held while an interpreter – often an English teacher – helped conduct an interrogation. Depending on the degree of paranoia prevalent in the country at the time, the direction of the political wind and the phase of the moon, the subject might be given a cup of ersatz coffee and an apology for any misunderstandings or worse, forced to relinquish his film and notes, with a stern warning to find a hobby less sensitive militarily. Detention by the *Transportpolizei, Milicija,* or in the direst circumstances, the secret police, could be humiliating, intimidating and downright frightening, given the brute power of the State. The country with the worst reputation for arrests and film confiscations was Yugoslavia, which British enthusiasts nick-named "You-no-go-slavia". Though the response ranged from farce to tragedy, the official attitude toward railway photography was almost universally negative: whether the image in the viewfinder was an East German Pacific, a Czech 4-8-2, a Rumanian Berk-

shire or a Soviet 2-10-0, the enthusiast was clearly engaging in espionage!

A German photographer was stopped on departing Czechoslovakia. This time the official was mildly apologetic: "I am sorry to have to take your film. You see, before 1968 (the year of the Soviet-led invasion) there would have been no problem." Incredibly, the film was developed and returned by mail! This case was a remarkable exception to the rule of detain and confiscate.

Certain photographers employed creative tactics of their own, from last-moment switching of an unexposed roll of film for an exposed one, to diving through the cab of a moving locomotive – to the astonishment of the crew – in order to evade the police. One American found that by flashing his Texaco Oil Company credit card – with its red star logo–and claiming to be an official of the American Communist Party, he could gain entry to several railroad yards in Leningrad and the Baltics, returning with images of Soviet steam in the snow. To photograph the last steam operations in Lithuania and Byelorussia, Huxtable made illegal side trips – including a cab ride in a 2-6-2 – away from official tourist routes, only to be arrested, interrogated, declared *persona non grata* and expelled. But the exposed film, hidden in a soiled towel, escaped detection. Ziel was allowed to take pictures at the Narva, Estonia engine shed in 1972, by handing out glossy prints and postcards from his 1970 Siberian foray. On his second trip to Hungary, the secret police took only the film in the camera, ignoring a half-dozen rolls marked "DR" (East Germany), but actually exposed in Hungary the previous three days. When asked why he had just one roll to show for his Magyar efforts, Ziel replied: "I shoot *quality*, not *quantity*." A Dutch enthusiast, wanting to see the last active P36 4-8-4s at Skovorodino, Siberia, made arrangements with a travelling companion to look after his luggage, stepped off the *Rossiya* and spent hours at the shed before being accosted by the police. He was taken to a hostel for drunks, where he was held until the arrival of the next westbound Train No. 1. To the local authorities, only a foreigner influenced by vodka would leave his warm compartment in the bitter chill of winter – and miss the train!

Fortunately, this "cat and mouse" game had its lighter moments. In 1974, a security-conscious but somewhat naive commuter informed Huxtable in Dmitrovgrad, Bulgaria: "I am making a citizen's arrest. Wait here while I fetch a policeman." Needless to say, the suspect boarded the next departing train. Riding the Trans-Siberian in 1970, Ziel was defended

Communist propaganda often was totally lacking in fact or logic, insulting the intelligence of local citizen and visitor alike. The three-storey-tall sign in East Germany in 1980 (upper left) depicting a 48-star American flag (more than twenty years out of date) on a bomb reads: "NATO – a dangerous treaty against peace." Far more pleasing to the eye was *Deutsche Reichsbahn* 2-8-2 No. 41 1033 (above) racing a passenger train at Seehausen, on October 1, 1974.

Two photos, Ron Ziel

Below, Nikolai Pytel

One Russian who managed to photograph Soviet steam in regular service was Andrei V. Kazachkov. As an engineer employed in railway work, he was able to convince the security *apparat* that the pictures were necessary for his job. Several of his photos appear in the Soviet Union chapter.

by his sleeping-car attendant, who kept police at bay while he photographed *her* train! On the same trip, a furious policeman ordered him to stand beside the first coach, which was full of soldiers going home on leave, while the chief was summoned. A sympathetic sergeant beckoned the photographer into the car where, in one compartment, six soldiers were playing cards. With his glasses removed and cameras stowed beneath the seats, Ziel was hastily draped in a Soviet Army greatcoat and visored hat, given a hand of cards and squeezed into a corner seat. Three red-faced policemen clambered aboard, the chief shouting "Amerikanski?" The sergeant shrugged, answering "Nyet Amerikanski." Train No. 1 was held up for ten minutes while the police searched *underneath* it, with the crew yelling at them to get out of the way. As a crowd gathered, the police stood perplexed. Aboard the departing *Rossiya*, the soldiers roared, patted their Cold War mascot on the back and poured vodka. So much for the power of the State, thousands of miles from the Kremlin.

By the 1980s, the situation was improving, partly because of the need for Western currency brought in by visitors, but also due to the breaking-down of Communist authority. Unfortunately, the collapse of the system in Eastern Europe came just as the age of steam was ending. But there was still China, as well as Vietnam and Cuba. In China, group tours soon were supplemented by individual travel; the array of fine photographs showing Chinese steam in action can only hint at what might have been obtained in the USSR a decade earlier, had Soviet policies been as liberal.

In the post-Communist era, the fascination with

11

Warszawa, dnia 2 września 1972 r

ZEZWOLENIE   Nr 38/72

Zezwala się Obywatelowi U S A

p. Ronowi Z I E L

- na wstęp i dokonywanie zdjęć fotograficznych lokomotyw parowych w obrębie w s z y s t k i c h D.O.K.P.

Wykonanie objętego zezwoleniem zadania może nastąpić po uprzednim zgłoszeniu się u Dyrektora właściwej terytorialnie O K P, który ustali miejsce i czas dokonywania zdjęć fotograficznych.

Zezwolenie ważne jest do dnia 31 grudnia 1972 r.

Po wykorzystaniu, zezwolenie należy zwrócić do Komendy Głównej Służby Ochrony Kolei.

Z-ca Komendanta Głównego SOK

(B. Olejniczak)

A blanket photo permit (above) was inadvertently issued by Polish authorities to Ron Ziel in September, 1972. It allowed unrestricted photography and resulted in a flurry of complaints from local and railway police to the Communications Ministry, issuers of the document and administrator of the Polish Railways. Later permits, when obtainable, were far more restrictive. Unfortunately, Ziel's itinerary was limited to just five days in Poland on that trip, while the permit was good for four months. When a large quantity of film was confiscated from a government-approved and guided railway tour group in Czechoslovakia in May, 1971, negotiations through the United States Department of State began immediately to retrieve the film. In October, 1972, co-author Ziel took custody of the film from the U.S. embassy in Prague, which had obtained it from the Czech Foreign Ministry, once the Interior Ministry grew bored playing with it. It was inventoried in Ziel's room at the Hotel Centrum (below) prior to being air-shipped directly to New York.

steam in the former "Socialist Republics" and in places where the red star still sputtered was as strong as ever. Enough classes of locomotives are represented by preserved examples in the former Soviet Union and in the erstwhile "Captive Nations" of the East Bloc to make a visit still rewarding. Locomotives, either singly or in multiples, are steamed for excursions, tours and commemorative events. There are steam festivals in the Czech Republic, *Plandampf* (steam engines hauling regular freight and passenger trains) in eastern Germany and steam tours in Russia and Ukraine; the latter providing photographic possibilities undreamed of by the authors when they first saw the P36 in 1970. What a pleasure it is to be able to point a camera at a blue-liveried three-cylinder Czech 4-8-4T or a green SZD 2-6-2 in the former USSR without having to hide behind a tree or look nervously over one's shoulder!

Aside from the sample "war stories" related, what of the locomotives themselves? They are all presented by country, beginning with Eastern Europe. The authors hope that readers will appreciate the rarity of many of these pictures and the trying, often threatening conditions under which they were taken. (Staring down the wrong end of an AK-47 assault rifle is not everyone's idea of a thrilling holiday experience.)

Undoubtedly, the survival of steam beneath the red star was prolonged by the austerity, bureaucracy and inefficiency of Communism, but the official inclusion of steam locomotives (some approaching their centenary) in the same strategic category as military bases and missile sites was a tragedy – for photographers and historians alike. In prohibiting railroad photography, each country concerned was preventing its own history from being recorded. Although, after thirty years of film confiscations, the various ministries for state security – from Budapest to Bucharest – must have collectively amassed enough material for a dozen volumes like this one!

Where the photographs do not exist, the memories of those few fortunate (and often foolhardy) enough to have made the attempt, remain. In any case, no picture can convey the excitement of lying awake in a berth on the *Rossiya*, listening as that wonderful P36 barked its twenty-car train away from a remote Siberian station stop, the sounds of its chime whistle, then the air horn, blasting into the clear, frosty night. That was an experience never to be forgotten – or confiscated!

-Nils Huxtable, Vancouver, Canada
-Ron Ziel, Water Mill, New York, USA

Reflecting the setting winter sun, Chinese Railways QJ 2-10-2s Nos. 1839 and 6231 worked a heavy freight at Mengjiawan, as they headed upgrade toward the horseshoe curves in January, 1992.   Pete Skelton

The most distinctive locomotive to run on the East German Railways into the early 1970s was streamlined Pacific No. 02 0201. In later years she was used for test purposes at Halle and occasionally in regular service; now the 4-6-2 is preserved and powers special trains.   Nils Huxtable

SOVIET UNION

In 1970, when the authors–then unknown to each other–first visited the USSR to photograph what little steam remained, they were almost too late. Steam's share of train-haulage had dwindled from over 94% in 1950 to about 60% in 1960, and to a mere 3.5 % by 1970. The elimination of steam traction had been planned for that same year, but those first glimpses of five-foot gauge, seventeen-feet-tall, roller-bearing, semi-streamlined 4-8-4s at the head of Train No. 1, the *Rossiya,* were proof enough that steam was not yet finished. The goals of the 1966-70 Five Year Plan had not been met, and pockets of steam were to linger on into the 1980s. The P36 Northerns on Trans-Siberian passenger trains, however, were the last significant Soviet mainline steam operations.

Until recently, 90% of all inland traffic in Russia moved by rail, and the Trans-Siberian Railway, pushed to completion by the Imperial Russian government in the early 1900s, remains the principal means of commerce and military transport. With no transcontinental highway and with only air routes to complement the railroad, the USSR of the early 1970s relied heavily on this vital link between Moscow and the Pacific. That the tracks skirted the borders of a then-hostile China made security all the more strict. When one of the authors thanked the station master in Khabarovsk for allowing pictures of P36s, he replied, "Had you been a Chinese with cameras, you would have been shot!" The strategic importance of the line, with armed guards posted at each end of even the smaller bridges, made photography next to impossible.

Given the emphasis on moving merchandise, freight locomotives (mainly ten-coupled) for the Soviet Railways (SZD) were erected in the thousands; passenger engines in the hundreds. The IS 2-8-4 numbered 640; the P36, just 251. (One exception was that maid-of-all-passenger work, the S/Su 2-6-2, which totalled 3,750.) Though ten-coupled engines also came from the U.S–2,800 Ye Class 2-10-0s–and Germany–1,200 captured *Kriegsloks* , Russian locomotive builders (re-located east of the Urals during World War II) were able to supply most of the country's needs in peace- and wartime. (The heroic efforts of Soviet Railways personnel, civilian workers and Red Army railway battalions during the "Great Patriotic War" were covered extensively in co-author Ziel's *Steel Rails to Victory.*)

Excluding those locomotives acquired as war reparations and the hundreds of 0-10-0s built in satellite countries, postwar Soviet steam construction totalled more than 8,000. By the end of 1956, Kolomna and Lugansk Works, responsible for the production of classes P36 and LV respectively, had ceased building steam in response to a party directive handed down in February of that year. Although the increased availability of refined oil, the completion of new power stations and the comparative savings of diesel and electric traction over steam power were all contributing factors, the decision to end steam contruction may have been based more on politics than on economics. In overruling Ways and Communications Minister L. Kaganovich, who had recommended building 6,000 new steam locomotives as part of the 1956-

Shining, brand-new Su 101-19 (left) posed in the snow in 1928, On Train No. 1, P36-0082 (above) was being serviced at twilight alongside one of the ornate brick water towers at Kharagun, in the Far East. The seven-second exposure was taken on November 17, 1970.

*"When the trains stop,
that will be the end."*
-V.I. Lenin

1960 Five Year Plan, Kremlin officials later admitted having been influenced by the rapid dieselization of U.S. railroads. For the enthusiast, the decline of Soviet steam was aggravated by the modern image projected by official propaganda, and it seemed pointless to seek permission to photograph something that no longer existed!

Those who went in search of Soviet steam operations in the mid-1970s risked losing their film *and* their freedom. Co-author Huxtable's articles published in the British journal *Railway Magazine* relate his harrowing encounters with the police and the KGB. These were later condensed and translated into Russian for publication in the December, 1990 issue of *Krokodil* ("Crocodile"), the famous Soviet satirical monthly, which ran an article entitled "Spy on the Tracks, the story of how an English photographer snapped top-secret Soviet objects." After relating the events leading to Huxtable's expulsion from the country, *Krokodil* closed with this observation: "Obviously, our daily existence has so distorted our consciousness that to understand these odd people (railway enthusiasts) was simply not given to us. But they called on us to improve ourselves. Come, let us begin with the steam buff Huxtable and let us say to him: 'Nils, come and teach us to love steam engines.' "

Nowadays, visiting railway photographers are not merely tolerated in the former USSR, they are welcomed, their whims indulged. . .aboard steam excursions pulled by up to fifteen different locomotives. For the veteran "steam spy," such treatment may take some getting used to (Double-headed P36s in the

viewfinder without the omnipresent threat of arrest seems like *borscht* without sour cream.). But what a change from the days of intrigue and interrogations!

Some Czarist-era O Class 0-8-0s survived into the last years of steam, including this well-maintained example (upper left). The modern 9P 0-6-0T was the most numerous tank engine class: No. 11213 (lower left) was at Vilnius, Lithuania in December, 1975. For decades, Soviet propaganda extolled equal employment rights for women. Too often, however, women could be seen doing the heavy, menial work, while men operated the machinery. One bitterly cold day in Irkutsk, the driver of 9P 0-6-0T No. 10159 (below), grinned from his warm cab while women aligned the switches. Believed to have totalled more than 2,000, the 9P was the only SZD tank engine produced in large numbers, from 1936 to 1957. The photo of this Ya 2-6-0 (above) dates back to the Bolshevik Revolution.

The 2-6-2 was the preferred passenger engine in Soviet Russia, Hungary and Yugoslavia. A few worked in Bulgaria, Rumania and Czechoslovakia, with the most modern designs in East Germany and Poland. The Russian Su Class, erected over a forty-year period ending in 1951, comprised more engines (3,750) than all other European 2-6-2s combined. Preserved Su 251-86 (below) steamed through a snow storm in the Carpathian Mountains near Voronenka, Ukraine on December 10, 1992. The friendly engine crew of Su 251-47 (upper left) was giving the photographer a cab ride when he obtained this photo at Svencionys, Lithuania on July 11, 1976. The train was off-limits to foreigners, and the trip culminated in his arrest, interrogation (for several days) and deportation! Still assigned to the *Leningrad Express* in March, 1975, Su 251-83 (lower left) was being turned at Vilnius a few months before being replaced by diesels and scrapped.

Opposite, Nils Huxtable

Below, Victor Hand

ЧЕРНІВЦІ

Russian locomotive policy consisted of constructing many units of the same design and employing them on a variety of duties, rather than building several specialized classes. Such was the case of the E Class 0-10-0, 13,500 of which were built between 1912 and 1955; by far the most numerous class of steam locomotive in the world. Used in freight, local passenger and shunting service, their versatility was an important consideration, especially during wartime motive power shortages. The final version, class Er, not only ran until the last days of steam, but in late 1993, returned to regular service in Ukraine, to alleviate Russia's curtailment of oil supplies. Er 712-61 (upper left) wheeled a local freight at Buzhaninovo, near Moscow, in 1987. Er 770-99 (above) and two classmates were switching the yard at Tchernovtsy, Ukraine on the night of February 22, 1994. The following day, Er 799-36 and 767-06 (left) emerged from a tunnel near Mikulitchin. Built in 1899, "Softsign" (Ь) 0-6-0T No. 9773 (below), working at Syzran, Russia in 1983, has since been preserved.

Lower left, Ron Ziel   Upper left, lower right, A.V. Kazachkov   Upper right, Ron Ziel; lighting by Victor Hand

Once the decision had been made, in the early 1950s, to upgrade long-distance passenger services, a light weight, yet larger, more powerful and faster design than the forty-year-old Su Class was needed. An experimental 4-8-4 introduced in March, 1950 had proven successful, and four years later, 250 additional engines were ordered. They gained fame in their waning years, when many Western visitors began riding the Trans-Siberian during the late 1960s. The next-to-last P36, No. 0250 (above), had just taken over Train No. 1 from sister 0126 at Skovorodino, in the Soviet Far East, on November 16, 1970. Inside his roomy, all-weather cab, the engineer of excursion locomotive P36-0218 (left) eased out the throttle. P36-0022 (below) stood ready to depart Bira in 1970. Action photos of the P36s in regular service are hard to come by; preserved examples must therefore convey the impression of these fabulous 4-8-4s at speed. *Perestroika*, the liberalization policy initiated by Mikhail Gorbachev, made possible these pictures of P36-0064 (upper right) near Kovel, Ukraine in 1989 and P36-0050 doubleheading with blue-liveried 0218 (lower right) on the river bridge at Stanishevka in February, 1994. Less than a decade earlier, such a picture would have resulted in the photographer's immediate arrest for espionage!

Three photos, Ron Ziel   Upper right, Günter Oczko   Lower right, Nils Huxtable

"Afterwards, whenever I thought of the Trans-Siberian Express, I saw stainless steel bowls of borscht spilling in the dining car of the Rossiya *as it rounded a bend on its way to Moscow, and at the curve a clear sight from the window of our green and black steam locomotive – from Skovorodino onwards its eruptions of steamy smoke diffused the sunlight and drifted into the forest so that the birches smoldered and the magpies made for the sky".*

-THE GREAT RAILWAY BAZAAR, by Paul Theroux

Seen from the train, a P36 (above) powered the *Rossiya* near Urusha, Siberia. Lazar Kaganovich, Minister of Ways and Communications of the USSR urged the construction of 6,000 steam locomotives during the 1956-1960 Five-Year Plan: "I am for the steam locomotive. I am against those who imagine that we shall have no steamers. It is a robust machine, stubborn, and will not give up. However, one should not idealize the steam engine. I should say straight out that although in the future the steam locomotive will remain, the leading locomotives will be electric and diesel." He was purged, largely because he had "stubbornly insisted on developing steam traction", according to the charges against him. Had Kaganovich prevailed, there probably would have been over a thousand 4-8-4s built. The last mainline steam engine, No. P36-0251 (upper right), posed in the factory yard. The lettering on it reads: "Last steam locomotive built at the V. V. Kuybyshev Works at Kolomna, 1869-1956." No. 10420 was the builder's number. With added sheet-metal above the cylinder, P36-0211 (below) took water at Zubariovo. P36-0050 and 0218 (opposite, bottom) stormed upgrade near Bystra, Ukraine with a Dzherelo tour on February 25, 1994.

Three photos, Ron Ziel

Above, Ian Button collection

Opposite, Ron Ziel

Above, Ian Button collection

Below, Reino Kalliomäki collection

Star of Soviet steam: P36-0250 (opposite) stood majestically at the head of Train No. 1. The twenty-minute Skovorodino engine-change offered a rare opportunity for photography on the Trans-Siberian. Except for the buffers and clerestory cab roof, the prototype of 640 IS (*Josef Stalin*) Class 2-8-4s (above) might have rolled out of Ohio's Lima Works. The tender of IS 20-1 (20-ton axle load) carries the slogan "There are no fortresses which the Bolsheviks could not storm!" in this 1933 photograph. The IS was actually a passenger version of the earlier FD 2-10-2, incorporating the same boiler, as well as other major components. After Stalin's death, the IS was re-classified FDp (*Felix Dzherzhinsky* - passenger); not much of an improvement, since Dzherzhinsky was the founder of the secret police! Only one 2-8-4 is known to survive, and it was mounted on top of a three-storey-tall pedestal in Kiev until Valentin Pashkevitch, director of Dzherelo, the Ukranian tour firm which runs private steam trains, traded another engine for it. The IS became the eighth in his expanding stable of operating mainline steam locomotives. Two hundred standard U.S. Army 2-8-0s were built especially for service on Soviet five-foot-gauge track as class Sh, a ('a' denoting 'American'). No. 127 (right) was the last G.I. Consolidation to operate at Talinn, Estonia where it posed with the yard and engine crews for this official 1960s photograph.

"Why were you photographing engines?"
"Because I am interested in railways."
"What do you mean — interested?"
"In my country many people spend their spare time watching and photographing locomotives. They sometimes travel hundreds of miles just to see a particular engine."
"You are a fool to expect me to believe that! Why should anyone want to study the engines of his own country? Besides, the police in Western countries would never allow people to spy on the railways."
- HOW GOOD ARE THE RUSSIANS
AT RAILROADING?
J.N. Westwood, TRAINS Magazine, August 1958

Upper left, upper right, Ron Ziel

In 1934, the first SO 17 (named for Sergo Ordzhonikidze; 17-ton axle load) was turned out. Together with a slightly heavier version (SO 18), about 5,000 were built, including an estimated 1,200 condensing engines which re-circulated the exhaust steam back to the tender, for use in desert regions. A development of the E Class 0-10-0, these small-wheeled Decapods ran until the end of steam: SO 17-2447 (lower left) was working at Leningrad (now St. Petersburg) in 1987. The cylindrical fuel tank in the tender of oil-burning SO 17-4371 is clearly visible as it leads coal-fired No. 3146 (upper left) across the massive bridge spanning the frozen Dnestr River near Kamyenetz-Podolski, Ukraine in 1994.

Despite the presence of armed guards and attack dogs, twenty-five photographers were unleashed without restrictions. In 1933, Beyer Peacock sent five large 0-4-0T shunters to the USSR; ('soft sign') No. 2137 (above) still served as Korosten, Ukraine shed pilot in 1994. The vastness of the Soviet Union and its official policy of secrecy regarding railroad operations meant that narrow-gauge lines (apart from children's Pioneer railways) were rarely seen by foreigners. A 1928 builder's photo shows 0-8-0 No. 20 (below), complete with hammer-and-sickle-embossed works plate.

Lower left, Reino Kalliomäki   Lower right, Ian Button collection

Above, Nils Huxtable

In the early 1930s, the Soviet Railways adopted a "big engine" policy, raising the axle-loading to twenty tons on upgraded lines, which were then capable of carrying heavier, more powerful locomotives. Turned out in November, 1931, the first design was a 2-10-2 built to American standards, including provision of a mechanical stoker. More than 3,200 of the FDs (*Felix Dzherzhinsky*) had been built by 1941, when production ceased. Since the heaviest mainlines were being electrified and dieselized in the late 1950s, the FDs became surplus, and over a thousand were sold to the Chinese (page 209), who re-gauged them.

FD 20-2714 doubleheaded with SO 17-3146 (below) on a Dzherelo special near Vinnitsa in 1994 and climbed out of the Dnestr River valley (lower right) in May, 1993. The 1,900 Lend-lease 2-10-0s sent from the U.S. during World War II to join 875 First World War sisters were used mainly in the Far East and Siberia. Erected by Baldwin in 1944, Ye 2449 (above) switched the yard at Yablonovaya on December 21, 1972. Taking photographs from trains in the USSR was strictly forbidden, so the 1970 view of Ye 3068 (upper right) from the *Rossiya* as it passed through Taldan would have been grounds for arrest.

Below and upper right, Ron Ziel

Lower right, Gunter Oczko

As the German Army advanced into the USSR in June, 1941, its locomotive requirements became acute, so more than 1,200 (perhaps hundreds more) of the standard wartime 52 Class 2-10-0s were assigned to the Eastern Front, including many built to the Russian five-foot gauge. The counterattacking Red Army captured large numbers of them, and more were acquired as *Trofiya* (war booty; hence the T Class designation) as the war ended. These included TE-5653 and 6115 (above), waved forward by a flagman at Stanishevka, Ukraine on February 20, 1994. Eight days later, a TE and an LV 2-10-2 (below) simmered in the snow at Tchors. It was so difficult to visit many areas of the USSR during Soviet times that neither co-author saw an LV Class 2-10-2, much less got the chance to photograph any of them, although 522 were built as the last mainline freight design between 1954 and 1956. Fortunately, several have been retained, and both authors had ample opportunities to obtain action pictures of LV-0202 (lower left) in February and March, 1994. Far to the north, near Arkhangelsk, LV-0233 (upper left) worked another excursion on July 17, 1992.

Upper left, Ian Button   Three photos, Ron Ziel

The most successful and numerous of the post-World War II SZD freight engine designs was the class P (*Pobyeda* or "Victory", for the year of its introduction: 1945), later re-classified L, after its chief designer, L.C. Lebedyanski. More powerful than the E 0-10-0 and the SO and Lend-lease Decapods, about 5,200 of these lightweight 2-10-0s were built. Since the Ls were so widespread, more photographs are available of them in regular service than of any other Soviet locomotives. In addition to appearing on page 1, the L gives an encore performance here. L-3767 (upper left) wheels a train of covered hopper cars. Another member of the class (lower left) is seen arriving at Narva, Estonia with a long freight from Leningrad in December, 1970. The oldest class to survive until the end of steam was the common, pre-revolutionary O (*Osnovnoi Tip*, or basic type) 0-8-0, which totalled about 8,000 by 1912. These engines were well-suited for shunting and industrial use; in this capacity, 0v-5804 (above) was still working at Lyubertsky, near Moscow, in 1976. Aside from three streamlined 4-6-4s built for the Leningrad-Moscow "Red Arrow" service, two 2-10-4 prototypes and a lone 2-6-6-2 mallet, the Soviets turned out two designs impressive even by American standards. One was a cumbersome 4-14-4; however, its long, rigid wheelbase of almost thirty-three feet kept spreading the rails and derailing the engine on curves, and it was scrapped after spending years in storage. The winter of 1954-55 saw the Soviet Railways' last steam design: a pair of 2-8-8-4 simple articulateds which proved too costly to maintain. In any case, they were soon made redundant by electrification. P38-0002 (below) at the Kolomna Works in January, 1955 and its twin were the largest (125 1/2 feet long) and heaviest (214.9 tons) locomotives ever built in the Soviet Union.

Upper left, D. Trevor Rowe   Lower left, Howard Serig (Ziel collection)   Above, A.V. Kazachkov   Below, Ian Button collection

HUNGARY

Opposite, Ron Ziel

Above, A. E. Durrant

In the 1970s, anyone who wanted to relive the thrill of standing in a railway station with three or four snorting steam trains lined up and waiting to set off had only to go to Hungary. Long gone of course, were the streamlined 4-4-4Ts and other equally exotic locomotives of the *Magyar Államvasutak* – Hungarian State Railways, but enough remained to occupy the time and the viewfinders of the railroad photographer, on what had once been among the greatest railway systems of Europe. The first private railroad had opened in 1846, and in 1868, the MÁV took over the independent lines. As part of the Austro-Hungarian Empire, all of Hungary's early locomotive designs were of Austrian origin; the first true Magyar engines appearing in 1893.

After the beginning of the 20th Century, Hungarian engineers began breaking away from the traditional Austrian approach to locomotive design. New 4-6-0 and 4-4-2 types were followed by 4-6-2s, greatly improving passenger service. In 1908, the MÁV began a long reliance on the Prairie-type in both tank engine and tender varieties; an ideal mixed-traffic engine for light mainline as well as branchline passenger service and freight work. When Hungary emerged defeated from both World Wars, it lost not only much territory, but also many locomotives (including entire classes) to its new neighbors. Thus the 2-6-2 remained the mainstay of MÁV steam-power until the end, serving the railways of Rumania and Yugoslavia as well.

Blasting out of one of the few tunnels in Hungary, 4-8-0 No. 424.007 (opposite) left a powerful impression on the photographer, who crouched in a narrow space between the retaining wall and the track. The smoke-deflectored engine, its big red star prominent, brightened a grey morning at Möcsény on February 12, 1979. The heaviest suburban locomotive design on MÁV was the class 442, a 2-8-2T with Brotan-type watertube firebox. 442.017 (above) rolls into Nyugati Station, Budapest, in 1963. Tank engines were ideal for the rapid start and stop suburban lines, the lack of a separate tender greatly improving visibility and obviating the need for turning the locomotive at the end of its run.

Apart from the 324 class 2-6-2, the one Hungarian locomotive which stands out in the minds of steam historians is the 424 class 4-8-0, dating from 1924. By 1940, a mere twenty-seven of these rugged and uncomplicated dual-service machines had been produced, because there had been no real demand for quantities of so powerful an engine. World War II changed that, and construction continued until 1958, by which time hundreds were in service... in Hungary, Yugoslavia, Czechoslovakia, the USSR and even in China. Towards the end of the steam era in Hungary, when photography restrictions were somewhat relaxed, the roster was dominated by the 424s and a few other classes: the 324 2-6-2, the 375 and 376 2-6-2T and the 411 2-8-0. The latter was the standard American Army World War II workhorse, 510 of which wound up in Hungary as the principal freight power. A few German 52 class Decapods were also to be seen, as well as stragglers from almost extinct classes and a few narrow-gauge operations.

37

The Hungarians were known for designing reliable, sturdy steam locomotives, building them in the hundreds over a few years' time, then dusting off the same blueprints, perhaps adding some modifications and resuming production two or three decades later. Such was the case with the light branchline 2-6-2T of class 376, first built in 1914. About 190 had been erected by 1923, including No. 376.461 (upper left), seen simmering at Kaposvár shed in the winter of 1979, when she was sixty-four years old. Approximately sixty more were built in the 1940s; one of them being No. 376.616 (upper right), also at Kaposvár on July 17, 1972. Appearing only a year after the 376-class was the heaviest of the 2-6-2T types: class 342, weighing seventy-one tons (compared to fifty-four tons for the 375s and a mere forty-five tons for the 376s). No. 342.234 (left) was leaving Györ, bound for Sopron on May 27, 1963. Between 1885 and 1900, 488 tall-stacked little 0-6-0Ts were built as the standard MÁV switcher. One of the last survivors, 377.027 (lower right), shunted an industrial siding at Ács on August 28, 1978, when this typically Austrian-appearing engine was over ninety years old. A much newer industrial-type locomotive was No. 490.057 (below) on the narrow-gauge Casbasci-Szob quarry line, on a damp, cool February morning in 1979. Built by Mávag of Budapest in 1950, she is shown hauling stone cars, enveloped by exhaust steam.

Top and bottom, Ron Ziel

Center, D. Trevor Rowe   Opposite page, Nils Huxtable

Above, Ron Ziel

Below, A. E. Durrant

Among the fascinating stragglers which survived into the final decade of Hungarian steam was 0-6-0 No. 370.011 (top left), built about 1899 and still hard at work switching a short mine branch at Nagymànyok eighty years later. Most of the 139 members of class 370 – built between 1898 and 1908 – were long gone, but this venerable veteran of two World Wars, Nazi and Soviet occupation and the 1956 popular counter-revolution plodded on faithfully. Another typically Austrian design was the MÁV class 326, dating from 1882, with outside frames; large, hinged smokebox doors; and a tall, flaring stack, similar to that of the 370s. Also a six-wheel shunter, No. 326.273 (above), was built in 1892; here, at the age of sixty-six, she does switching chores at Budapest Nyugati Station, with a modern Russian passenger car behind, on August 22, 1958. Perhaps the longest-running period of construction of a virtually identical series of locomotives – fifty-two years – was that of the 375 class 2-6-2Ts. The first were built in 1907 as saturated engines, later production runs being superheated. After more than 700 had been produced, the final batch appeared in 1959, the last year of Hungarian steam production. No. 375.684 (right) worked a branchline local at Ravazd, on October 28, 1972, and sister 375.688 (upper right) slowed for a station stop at Kismegyer the following day. Identical sisters appear in the Rumanian and Yugoslav chapters.

40

The finest in Magyar steam was the 424-class 4-8-0; originally built without the large smoke deflectors (page 127), the 424 was greatly improved by them, taking on a rakish, racy look. Hungarian engineers were inventive and, not satisfied with the Giesl form of exhausting steam, came up with their own Ister system. On the 4-8-0s the double-chimney version was used. While most of the 424 class remained on the MÁV, others were sold abroad or given as war reparations; a number of the latter later being returned, so the exact total and disposition of the 4-8-0s is impossible to determine. No. 424.090 (upper left), with red running gear and star, posed at Györ on August 28, 1978. No. 424.198 (lower left) easily handled a twelve-car passenger train in the same area four years earlier. In a steamy simultaneous departure (above), a pair of Twelve-wheelers leave the capital on a cool morning in 1963. With a high-pitched boiler, firebox above the driving wheels and "elephant-ear" smoke deflectors, 424.127 (below) looked powerful and sleek as she worked a passenger train at Baja in 1979. When the Secret Police were questioning one of the authors, who had been arrested for photographing the 4-8-0s, the interrogator proudly informed him that these locomotives had won awards of design excellence in the 1920s. Then the serious questioning resumed!

Lower left and below, Ron Ziel   Upper left, Nils Huxtable   Above, A. E. Durrant

Above, D. Trevor Rowe

The Hungarians made good use of several classes of 4-6-0s, all of which were built for speed; riding on large diameter slender-spoked driving wheels. Most of them were striking in appearance. Unfortunately, they were extinct by the 1970s, so few good photographs are available; some of the finest are shown here. The 302 class, dating from 1910, came from the Austrian Südbahn following World War I. Fourteen went to the MÁV, including No. 302.609 (above), accelerating an express train at Ersci on May 30, 1963. Another ex-Austrian 4-6-0 type was the 329 class, coming to Hungary via Czechoslovakia (ČSD Class 363.0) after the Second World War. No. 329.507 (right), sporting a toy train-like Vanderbilt tender salvaged from a scrapped 4-4-2, backed

through the yard at Nyíregyháza in 1961. With a conical smokebox door and V-fronted cab, smoke deflectors and cowled Pecz-Rejto water purifier behind the dome, Ten-wheeler No. 328.021 (lower left), seen at Budapest in 1963, was one of 141 such handsome engines to be delivered to MÁV in the 1918-1922 period. Eighty-three were constructed by Henschel of Germany and fifty-eight in Budapest, seventeen additional Henschels going to Czechoslovakia as reparations. With the driving rods working the lead pair of coupled wheels instead of the usual center set, the 140 4-6-0s built just prior to World War I included No. 327.139 (lower right), in charge of thirteen four-wheel cars at Miskolc, on May 10, 1961.

Three photos, A. E. Durrant

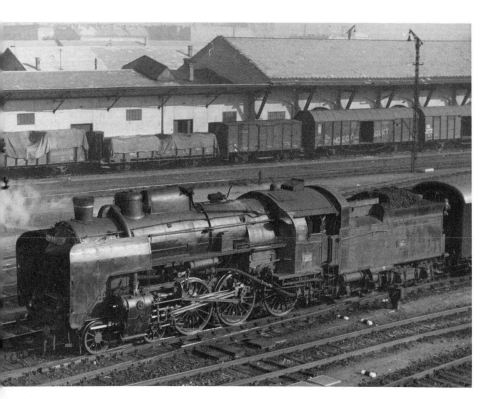

44

Even as the Germans were constructing more than 6,500 identical 52 class 2-10-0 *Kreigslokomotiven* (war locomotives) between 1942 and 1945, the Americans were building 2,120 S-160 2-8-0s for use in the war effort. With the defeat of the Axis powers, all of the chunky Consolidations became surplus, although many were brand-new and none more than three years old. There would have been little use for them in the United States, since most American railroads had already begun to dieselize and the steam locomotives still being ordered were mostly large super-power machines, not small 2-8-0s. Nearly half of the S-160s found roundhouses in just two Eastern European countries: 510 in Hungary and 500 in Poland, where they became the standard freight-power in the former nation and mostly switch engines in the latter; working into the 1980s in both countries. On the MÁV, the last concentration of them was at Hatvan, where No. 411.155 (upper left) was having her fire cleaned as a sister shunted boxcars on the adjoining track. On the same day – February 13, 1979 – the photographer, without permission as usual, lugged his big 4- by 5-inch Speed Graphic camera into the Hatvan engine terminal. After he took the picture of No. 411.170 slowly moving out past No. 411.227 (above), the two men in front of No. 424.354 began shouting as they ran towards him, so he headed out of the yard. Simultaneously, 411.227 began following the first 2-8-0; the only time that the photographer had ever been pursued by men both on foot and in locomotives! On a cold, clear December 5, 1970, No. 411.441 (left) was silhouetted by the low winter sun at Nagykáta as she hauled a cut of ore cars tender-first. Often, these locomotives wore large red stars painted on their smokebox doors; their United States Army Transportation Corps Lima or Baldwin builder plates a mere four feet away. Such were the contradictions in the lands of steam beneath the red star!

Three photos, Ron Ziel

47

Early in the streamlined era, the MÁV designed and built a pair of completely streamlined 4-4-4 tank engines in 1936, followed by two more in 1939. Unique in appearance and capable of 100 mph, Nos. 242.004 and 242.003 (above) powered the *Balt-Orient Express* into Budapest in September, 1963. At a number of locations during the Cold War, locomotives passed through the Iron Curtain on a regular basis. Like every other East European country, Hungary had its share of German 52 class *Kriegsloks*, such as No. 520.030 (below), shown at Wiener Neustadt, Austria in January, 1972, prior to returning to home rails. Between 1909 and 1923, the MÁV ordered a total of 895 324 class 2-6-2s and twenty years later added nearly 100 more. Although hundreds were lost after the break-up of the Austro-Hungarian Empire and following World War II as reparations, enough remained on the MÁV to bolster the steam fleet until the end. Two of the latter series are shown in their most common role as branchline maids-of-all-work: No. 324.1559 (upper right) in passenger service at Galgamarsa, and No. 324.1581 (lower right) with a freight at Galgaguta on October 30, 1972.

POLAND

During the 1970s, Poland was the steamiest country in Europe. Though dieselization and electrification had thinned the once 4,000-strong fleet, steam's share of passenger and freight train mileage was still impressive. Indeed, the sheer quantity of steam was the reason many enthusiasts came to Poland, both to travel around the country behind 2-8-2s, 2-10-0s, 2-6-2s, 2-8-2Ts and 4-6-0s, and to explore one steam-filled roundhouse after another. Amazingly, the official end of steam – timed to coincide with the 150th anniversary of Poland's first railway (1845) – may never take place. By 1993, the steam total was down to 123, but the authorities have apparently decided to continue steam operations at Wolsztyn, near the German border, and to establish other steam centers; the latest being Chabowka, on the Kraków-Zakopane line.

Poland ceased to exist as an independent nation between 1795 and 1919, so the first 75 years of its railroad history were dominated by the powers that had occupied it, built its railways and supplied the locomotives. The new *Polski Koleja Panstwowe* (PKP) – Polish State Railways – set about resolving its inherited problems; chief priorities were to re-gauge the Russian trackage and to establish a locomotive industry.

At first, consolidation and standardization were difficult, the PKP having acquired ten separate systems of seven different gauges! After World War I, the Poles received 175 of the American military "Pershing" 2-8-0s, along with Austrian and Prussian engines, to alleviate the acute motive power shortage until new designs could be mass-produced.

In 1920, the PKP developed a complex classification system based on a locomotive's duty, wheel arrangement, type – whether tender or tank engine, year of introduction and origin. P (*Pospieszny*) indicated express passenger; 0 (*Osobowy*), mixed passenger and light freight; and T (*Towarowy*), freight. Thus, a Ty-23 was a freight 2-10-0 (y) built in 1923 (23). The 0k1-27 was a mixed (0) tank engine (k) of the 2-6-2 type (1), introduced in 1927 (27). The k meant *kusy* – Polish for truncated. The 2 in Ty-246 revealed its foreign (i.e. American) design and order date: 1946. Interestingly, there was no separate designation for switch engines, probably because few locomotives in Poland were designed specifically for shunting; rather, older road power was downgraded to yard duties.

With limited resources, the PKP adhered to a policy of keeping locomotive construction basic. In the past, German designs had predominated; German influence, emphasizing simplicity and reliability, were to characterize every PKP class. Following the Nazi invasion in September, 1939, most of the PKP was absorbed into the *Deutsche Reichsbahn* (DRG). In turn, many DRG locomotives were transferred east, especially after the attack on Russia in June, 1941. By 1945, Poland lay in ruins, its cities and railroads ravaged by the retreating Germans and the advancing Soviets. When the postwar map of Europe was redrawn and Poland moved 100 miles westward, the PKP took over the railways of East Prussia, Pomerania and Silesia, along with hundreds of DRG locomotives. In the east, however, the Russians appropriated many Polish engines. To augment the PKP roster, hundreds of new and almost-new American locomotives of both military and non-military origin were sent – just before the Iron Curtain imprisoned half of Europe.

Even during the final twenty years of large-scale steam operations, it was possible to see the entire period of Polish locomotive design, from 1923 to

1951, represented by 2-10-0s and a host of other types, as well as American and German engines. Unfortunately, recording them on film was often frustrated by the insecurity and paranoia of Stalinism – Polish style. In 1972, for example, despite having an official permit for railway photography, co-author Ziel was stopped repeatedly by the black-uniformed railway police (SOK), many of whom telephoned the Ministry of Communications in Warsaw to verify the authenticity of the document (page 12). By contrast, many Polish railwaymen went out of their way to be helpful. In 1981, during the heady days of Solidarity, a letter from the Warsaw Railway Museum – written in English – was all co-author Huxtable needed to persuade the Kłodzko shed foreman, who spoke only Polish and German, to position half the allocation (one engine at a time) on the turntable for photogaphy! No permit? No problem.

Permits and organized steam tours notwithstanding, the political triumphs of Solidarity came too late for most enthusiasts. Even in *1993*, photographers were regarded with suspicion in certain areas; a few were still being arrested. As one British railway periodical wryly commented, anyone nostalgic for the Cold War steam experience had only to visit Poland!

Casting a long shadow across the tender of No. 01-49 79 (opposite), a young fireman begins his day's work as he climbs into the cab of his big 2-6-2 in the glinting light of sunrise at Sierpc. Two members of the most common of all classes of German locomotives in Poland rest in the cool last night of Summer at Malbork (the former German city of Marienburg), on September 20, 1974 (below). Ex-*Deutsche Reichsbahn* 52-class *Kriegslok* 2-10-0 No. Ty-2 544 and Prussian P 8 4-6-0 No. Ok-1 247 simmer between dwindling assignments in the old brick German roundhouse.

Two photos, Ron Ziel

For local and branchline passenger duties, the Prussian P8 – both in its original form as Class Ok-1 and the Polish version (Class 0k-22), with larger cab and firebox and high-pitched boiler – served the PKP between World War I and the end of steam. The 0k-22 was the first new PKP passenger type. Five engines were delivered by Hanomag in 1922; an additional 185 were produced by Chrzanów in the 1928-34 period. A few survived into the early 1980s, including 0k-22 17 (below) at Jaworzyna on July 21, 1976 and at Kedzierdzyn (lower right)

two years later. Former DRG P8s were acquired in large numbers as a result of German territory and locomotives ceded to Poland after both World Wars; others were acquired as reparations. In September, 1974, Poznań was teeming with Ok-1s. With one coupled to each end of a suburban train, as a third 4-6-0 accelerated from the main station (above), the PKP utilized an original steam version of the "push-pull" concept! A shining, freshly-painted Ok-1 70 (upper right), was about to depart from Ostrołeka on October 11, 1972.

Below, Pete Skelton

Above, upper right, Ron Ziel   Lower right, Nils Huxtable

Two of the most widespread postwar PKP classes were the Pt-47 2-8-2, of which 180 were built, and the Tkt-48 2-8-2T, totalling 194. The Pt-47 was essentially an improved Pt-31, a passenger Mikado of 1932; welded steel inner firebox, enclosed cab and stoker were some of the refinements. Assigned to expresses and locals on non-electrified lines, the Pt-47s crossed the border into East Germany at Görlitz and Frankfurt/Oder and reached Brest, in the former Soviet Union, hauling heavy international through trains, some of them composed entirely of Soviet Railways sleeping cars. At Poznań on September 25, 1974, prototype Pt-47 1 and sister No. 23 (left) were ready for departure. Equipped with the small smoke deflectors fitted to many classes beginning in 1949, the Tkt-48, though originally designed as a light-tonnage freight engine, soon proved suitable for branchline and suburban services. Tkt-48 2 (upper left) awaited a snowy departure from Pyskowice on February 24, 1979, while Tkt-48 28 (above) left Modlin with a Warsaw commuter train on October 12, 1972. Outside an army base near here, co-author Ziel set up his camera. First, two sentries puzzled over his permit, their commanding officer becoming more uncomfortable with the approach of every 2-8-2T. Finally, he *requested* that the photographer leave the area. Security forces would not have been so polite.

A FRIENDLY MEETING
OF FORMER ENEMIES

Well over 2,000 wartime DRG 2-10-0s – more than 1,900 of them being the lightweight 52 Class (15.2 tons axle-load) – were taken into PKP stock after 1945. The heaviest German Decapods, however, with an axle-load of almost twenty tons, were the three-cylinder 44 Class; sixty-seven joined the PKP roster. In addition, 486 U.S. Army S-160 2-8-0s were sent to Poland to replace locomotives destroyed or damaged. The PKP classified the 52s Ty-2, the 44s, Class Ty-4, and the American 2-8-0s, Tr-201 and Tr-203. While G.I. Tr-203 229 (right) drifted past with a transfer freight, former German Ty-4 109 blasted out of Malbork yard in September, 1974. Still active thirty years after the battles in which both engines had served as enemies – one escaping submarine attacks during the Atlantic crossing, the other evading the wrath of Allied bombing raids – the old war engines were working side by side. Within a few years, however, they were retired, dieselization and electrification having reduced steam activity still further. One of the busiest centers left was Nysa, where on August 15, 1979, 2-8-2T No. Tkt-48 144 (below) stormed out of the station with a local that included four bi-level articulated commuter cars. The following day, Pt-47 2-8-2 74 (lower right) tackled the climb westward from Nysa with an express for Kłodzko. Possessing an official photo permit also brought out the natural hospitality of Polish railway personnel; co-author Ziel being invited to spend every night in railway guest houses free of charge, with complimentary meals included.

Below, both photos, Nils Huxtable   Above, Ron Ziel

All three major American builders turned out the 2,120 G.I. 2-8-0 Army engines during the 1942-1945 period, as evidenced by the trio shown here on the PKP; the one on the previous page a graduate of Alco's Schenectady Works and the pair on this page from Baldwin and Lima. No. Tr-203 343 (above), was trundling down a track behind the big roundhouse at Pyskowice, with the lady fireman, Sofia Wasylów, leaning out of the cab on September 26, 1974. Many Polish locomotives were retired and scrapped right at the sheds where they last worked, as was the

Tr-203 (below), at Poznań, with major components already cut away and asbestos lagging flaking off the boiler and littering the ground. Only a few tracks away, three German locos – Ty-5 and Ty-2 2-10-0s and an Ok-1 4-6-0 – were still in steam, but they, too, would soon fall before the scrappers' torches. In 1928, the PKP introduced the heaviest 2-6-2 tank engine in Europe, class 0k1-27. Weighing 82 tons, 122 were built by 1933. No. 0k1-27 67 (opposite), accelerated a local passenger train away from Pyskowice station in 1974.

Three photos, Ron Ziel

The 01-49 2-6-2 was designed to replace the Ok-1 and 0k-22 4-6-0s (as well as the Austrian 2-6-2s) on local and secondary services, in much the same way as the DR and DB 2-6-2s were intended as P 8 replacements. The 01-49s ranged throughout the country, even handling expresses. The final passenger design, 116 01-49s were built. They could still be photographed in the 1990s, on local passenger runs out of Wolsztyn. Some of the high-drivered 2-6-2s were shedded at Sierpc, where 01-49 97 (above) awaited her next assignment on the night of September 23, 1974. The following day, 01-49 42 (below) departed with an express for Brodnica. In August, 1974, 01-49 73 (upper left) wheeled a train out of Olstyn. The wing-type smoke deflectors first used on this class were fitted to the Tkt-48s, Ty-51s and other classes. An American-built Ty-246 2-10-0 (lower left) pulled a heavy freight out of Toruń on August 8, 1974. These huge engines helped ease the motive power shortage on the war-battered PKP.

Upper and lower left, Nils Huxtable   Above and below, Ron Ziel

Above, Ron Ziel

The first true Polish design, the Ty-23 2-10-0, which went into production in 1923, was also the only Polish class fitted with a Belpaire firebox. Intended for heavy coal train service, 612 engines came from German, Belgian and Polish builders. Of those Ty-23s taken by Russia and converted to broad gauge, some were evacuated to the Turk-Sib Railway in Asia! A few broad gauge PKP Ty-23s were based at interchange yards on the Soviet border. Ty-23 226 (above) was switching Pyskowice yard in 1974. Introduced in 1946, the Ty-45 2-10-0s had "bath-tub" tenders copied from the 52 Class. Ultimately, 448 Ty-45s were produced, augmenting several thousand Polish and German Decapods. On July 3, 1961, Ty-45s 65 and 423 (below) doubleheaded a heavy mixed freight near Konin. The Ty-45 was almost identical to the prewar Ty-37, an improved version of the old Ty-23. Only twenty-seven had been constructed before the Nazi invasion; ten more followed just after it. Had the war not intervened, hundreds more would probably have been built.

Below, D. Trevor Rowe

German 2-10-0s were an overwhelming presence on the PKP. Beginning in 1940, the DRG, after absorbing most of Poland's railways, began producing standard Decapods in the hundreds. In addition to inheriting many 52 Class (Ty-2) and some 42 Class (Ty-3) 2-10-0s, the PKP also received, during the occupation, brand-new locomotives of both classes. Ty-43s 13 and 107 (above) at the Poznań roundhouse (along with Ty-45 359), were DRG 42s built new for the PKP. Also specially-constructed was Ty-42 103 (below), joined by Ty-45 325 and Ty-23 137 in the Pyskowice engine terminal. One of only fourteen known ex-DRG 50 Class 2-10-0s on the PKP was Wagner-deflectored Ty-5 1 (right) based at Poznań.

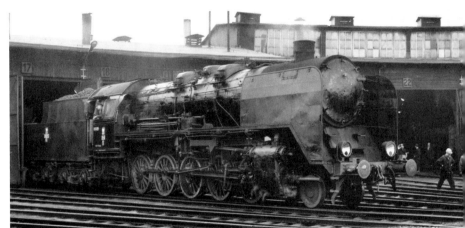

Three photos, Ron Ziel

Although intended for freight service, the Ty-2s also worked local passenger trains and shunted the yards. On a clear September morning in 1974, Ty-2 591 was being turned at the Malbork roundhouse (above) while a maintenance crew worked on Ok-1 4-6-0 No. 51, which had been partially moved out of its stall. After waiting for a clear signal, Ty-2 1217 (opposite) eased her freight from Brodnica into the yard at Sierpc. The main line to Toruń is in the foreground. Night photography of locomotives often intrigued, confused and sometimes frightened the local railwaymen. On the night of October 11, 1972,

with Ty-2 124 and 1077 (below) ready to leave Warsaw's Gdańsk freight yard, the photographer realized his first flash would bring both crews running and ruin the picture. At the tender of the second engine, one bulb drew the engineer and fireman to the cab window. The next flash temporarily blinded both men; the crew of the lead engine were similarly dealt with. By the time the men had regained their vision, this photo was completed. The startled crewmen read the photo permit, studied the flash equipment, shook hands with the delighted intruder and returned to their 2-10-0s.

Three photos, Ron Ziel

89
4

One of the largest tank engines in Europe was the powerful Okz-32 2-10-2T. Twenty-five were turned out by Cegielski in 1934-36, to handle heavy suburban trains as well as expresses around Zakopane, in the Carpathian mountains. A number were taken by the Soviets and never returned. Okz-32 11 (above) was at Krakow-Plaszow on July 22, 1964. Among the many Prussian designs on the PKP were the G 8 0-8-0s; long after those on the DB and DR had been withdrawn, No. Tp-4 148 (upper left) still served the Silesian Sand Railway at Pyskowice on August 11, 1980. Despite the mass closures of narrow gauge lines, a few were preserved, including a 75 cm. gauge peat-hauling operation: Kp-4 0-8-0 No. 469 (lower left), built in 1950, headed a passenger train at Verka. Among the more attractive Polish designs were the Pyskowice shed foreman's secretary (below left), recording the coal consumption of Ty-45 25, and the Poznań turntable operator (below right), both of whom added considerable interest to the photographer's steam itinerary. Although dimensions were noted, it was not considered discreet to ask about builder's dates.

Above, A.E. Durrant

Opposite: above, Nils Huxtable; below, T. Bray   Two photos below, Ron Ziel

In addition to the ex-U.S. Army 2-8-0s turned over to the PKP following the war, thirty "Liberations" were built by Britain's Vulcan Foundry as Class Tr-202. Many were working around Wrocław (formerly Breslau), including Tr-202 18 (above) on July 17, 1964. Before the Iron Curtain descended, Poland received 100 massive 2-10-0s from Baldwin, Lima and Alco in 1947. The most powerful engines seen in the country, they were somewhat restricted by their twenty-ton axle-load. Even so, Ty-246 27 (below), at Malbork in 1974, and her sisters im-

pressed PKP operating staff with their steam capacity and 58,200 pounds tractive effort. The PKP's version of the "Truman" engines was the Class Ty-51. Poland's last new steam locomotives, 232 were built by Cegielski between 1953 and 1957. A comparison of Ty-246 27 and Ty-51 57 (lower-right) at Modlin in 1972 shows their similarities. Indeed, the Ty-51, at 112 tons, weighed just four tons less than its American counterpart. Standing at the Olsztyn water tower, Ty-51 165 (upper right) waited to back into the locomotive depot.

Above, A.E. Durrant

Two photos below, Ron Ziel   Upper right, D.J. Short

Since the 2-8-2 type proved adequate for PKP express passenger requirements, fewer Pacifics were needed. The Pm-36, though high-drivered engines capable of 90 miles per hour, were the only 4-6-2s designed in Poland; Chrzanów built only two in 1937. The other PKP Pacifics were ex-DRG "reparations" engines: nine 03 10s and a number of O3s, including Pm-2 34 (left), leaving Toruń for Bydgoscz in April, 1975. So complete was the Nazi takeover of Poland in 1939 that most PKP locomotives were appropriated by the *Reichsbahn*, which transferred some to Germany and other parts of the Third Reich. A number of PKP engines were destroyed during the war; others were taken by the Soviets, including twenty Pt-31 2-8-2s based at Lvov (formerly in Poland, now in Ukraine). To fill the void, the roster was brought up to strength with the 586 American engines previously mentioned and thousands of ex-DRG locomotives. Note "the familiar shape of a German Class 86 in its less-familiar guise as PKP Tkt-3 31 in the yards at Poznań in 1964" (lower left), as described by A.E. Durrant. The PKP rostered forty-four of these. Of the 528 Prussian T18 4-6-4Ts built between 1912 and 1927, a number also remained in Poland: Oko-1 28 (below) was in commuter service at Poznań on July 25, 1964. At least one Oko-1, along with an example of almost every other class, has been preserved. Some exhibits in the PKP's vast collection are displayed at the outdoor railway museum in Warsaw; operational "heritage" engines are kept at steam centers such as Wolsztyn and Chabowka, where they are employed on timetabled trains and excursions. Unlike many Western countries (most notably, the United States), Poland is an outstanding example of enlightened steam preservation.

Continued steam operation was still very much in doubt as late as 1991, as THE WALL STREET JOURNAL related in a feature article on November 14th of that year. The PKP management had no desire to keep steam running, despite the rising number of Western photographers who were spending hard currency to experience the last regular-service standard-gauge steam in Europe. Much credit for changing the attitude of the bureaucracy must go to a PKP official at the Warsaw headquarters, Jerzy Wasilewski, who told the JOURNAL reporter: "Our chiefs think steam is out of mode. This is Communist mentality! From Rumania they order diesels. From Rumania I wouldn't order a frying pan!" The article also described how the PKP had employed a unique method of scrapping its unwanted steam power—not with expensive acetylene gas, but with explosives left over from the Cold War! " 'Have a look at this,' says Witold Wojtkowiak, master of the maintenance shed in Wolsztyn, passing a snapshot across his desk. It shows a field strewn with steam engines looking like exploded clocks. 'Mass liquidation,' he says. 'They use dynamite to get rid of them.' PKP has blown up 800 in the past year. That leaves 250..." Wojtkowiak saw a chance to charge Westerners to take pictures, observing that not long ago "they would have been arrested as spies."

At one time, there were nearly 2,800 kilometers of narrow gauge in Poland, principally 75 cm. Poland's territorial gains in the west added a number of German *Schmalspurbahnen* and locomotives to those acquired from privately-owned companies following the war. In recent years, however, most of the once-extensive network of sixty-eight narrow gauge routes has been closed. In 1993, only two steam-operated lines were left: Sroda-Zaniemysl and Gniezno-Powidz. On July 13, 1976, the Znin Wåsk roundhouse (above) stabled three different classes: Py-4 741, T-2 71 and Tx-26 422. One of numerous industrial narrow gauge lines was that serving the factory yards at Kazimierza Welke, where 0-6-0T No. 1521 (below) with auxiliary tender shunted a freight on October 13, 1972.

Built by Chrzanów in 1931, Pxa 2-8-0 No. 1811 (top) worked past an old boxcar serving as the station at Vrków in 1972. The standard postwar narrow gauge engine was a hefty 0-8-0, Class Px-48, examples of which were also exported to China. The fate of most Polish narrow gauge lines befell the 25 km. Warsaw-Radzymin suburban route alongside Highway E 12. Px-48 1914 (above) had the melancholy chore of hauling a rail recovery train on September 25, 1974. That same morning, Px-48 1758 (left) headed a packed commuter train out of Krosniewice. Both the narrow gauge and PKP steam were sinking into decline, along with the Communist system which had sustained them well past obsolescence.

73

Upper left, upper right, Ron Ziel

EAST GERMANY

The *Deutsche Demokratische Republik* (D.D.R.), or East Germany, was second only to Poland in its widespread use of steam when other European railroads were being overrun by diesels. Ironically, the survival of DR steam had its roots in the partition of Germany following World War II, when the railway system was divided into three parts: the western lines became the *Deutsche Bundesbahn* of the Federal Republic; East Germany retaining the *Reichsbahn* name, the eastern lines being absorbed into the PKP and the SZD. The now truncated *Deutsche Reichsbahn* (German State Railway), severely damaged by the war, was stripped by the Soviets, who exacted reparations by appropriating locomotives, as well as by de-electrifying and singling two-track mainlines. Limited to providing basic services, the DR could ill-afford new engines, and when post-war steam production ceased in 1960, only 332 had been built, in contrast to other East Bloc countries such as Czechoslovakia, which had produced them in large numbers. The famed Orenstein & Koppel Works (renamed Karl Marx by the Communists) then went over to diesel production. Many modifications were made by both the DB and the DR to the classes they shared, but it was the latter, forced by economics to curtail new steam

D. Trevor Rowe

construction, that began a massive rebuilding program, prolonging the lives of many locomotives. The standard, all-welded boiler fitted to new 2-6-2 and 2-10-0 designs was also used in the reconstruction of three older 2-10-0 classes, with a slightly larger version used to upgrade 4-6-2s and 2-8-2s. New cylinders, plate frames, Heinl feedwater heaters and Walschaerts valve gear became standard as well. The Giesl ejector, virtually untried in West Germany, was fitted to more than 500 *Reichsbahn* coal-burners. Indeed, the DR achieved a degree of steam locomotive standardization and availability unmatched by any other European railway.

Coinciding with the rebuild program – and a significant contribution to it – was a series of experiments, some of which involved conversions so radical, they were actually new designs. Two French Railways war orphans, a 231E 4-6-2 (DR Class 07) and a 241A 4-8-2 (DR Class 08), were extensively modified and converted to coal dust-firing (East Germany had substantial brown coal deposits.), along with a Prussian P4 4-4-0 and thirteen Prussian S10 4-6-0s. The first new DR locomotive, a solitary 25 Class 2-10-0, was similarly treated, as were twenty-nine 52 Class and twenty-two 44 Class Decapods.

For brake- and high-speed testing purposes, two Saxon XXHV 2-8-2s (Class 19, later 04) were reboilered, fitted with new cylinders and motion, and Riggenbach counter-pressure brakes. Based at the Halle Test Plant and later converted to oil-firing, they were withdrawn in 1976. Best-known among enthusiasts, however, were two very different semi-streamlined 18 Class (later 02) Pacifics: No. 201, transformed from 61 Class 4-6-6T No. 61 002; and No. 314, a former Baden S 3/6. Also later modified to burn oil, they handled both test and scheduled trains. Taken out of service in 1971, No. 02 0314 was sold to West Germany. Still used on excursions, No. 02 0201 (page 13) is credited with a maximum speed of 110 miles per hour attained on the ČSD's Prag-Velim test track in 1964.

With the notable exception of the Pacific-type passenger engines, DR motive power generally lacked the beauty and elegance of some of the locomotives of other rail systems in Eastern Europe. Even so, DR engines were generally more pleasing esthetically than their DB counterparts. Locomotive afficionados were fascinated by the different approaches used by the two German railways in both the re-building of existing types and the design of similar new ones. Unlike other Eastern European countries, the D.D.R. – and West Germany – received few foreign engines as the result of two world

wars and their ensuing reconstruction periods. In fact, the two Germanys not only had to return virtually all of the locomotives appropriated from occupied countries, but also lost thousands more as reparations. The quick repair of war-damaged engines, plus restoration of the factories which had produced them, averted serious shortages.

Unfortunately, rebuilding and experimentation could do little to lower the cost of locomotive fuel, which had always been a problem for East Germany. As the economic situation worsened, the DR began to extend mainline electrification, releasing diesels to replace steam. In the early 1980s, the U.S.S.R. began requiring payment for oil in hard currency. This was both a blow and a boon for steam: all remaining oil-fired standard gauge engines were withdrawn, whereas coal-fired locomotives – including classic Pacifics built in 1930 – were given a reprieve. In fact, standard gauge DR steam outlived steam on the DB by eleven years, and the last official revenue runs occurred in 1988, shortly before the fall of the Berlin Wall. But by then, steam enthusiasts were already sponsoring *Plandampf* events and specials. Meanwhile, the DR's narrow gauge lines, while drastically pruned during the 1960s and '70s, had fared better than those in Poland. In the 1980s, some 2-10-2Ts were completely rebuilt with new boilers, cylinders and frames. Thus, some regularly-scheduled steam operations in the former East Germany may continue beyond the year 2000.

East German contrasts. One of the Cold War "corridor" trains from Hamburg races through the West Berlin suburb of Grunewald behind Pacific No. 01 0519 (opposite, top) on December 14, 1970. The former Saxon State Railways used Meyer 0-4-4-0T compounds on both standard and narrow gauge lines. Built just prior to World War I by Hartmann for the steeply-graded and twisting Windberg branch near Dresden, the last of fifteen four-cylinder 98 0s (opposite, bottom) was at Freital-Potschappel in May, 1963. Ninety-six narrow gauge IV K Class Meyers were built between 1892 and 1921. No. 99 1606 (above) trundled through the woods at Streckewalde, on the Wolkenstein-Jöhstadt line, in 1980. In the early 1950s, the DR and DB each designed a 2-8-4T to replace life-expired Prussian and Saxon engines. DR No. 65 1067 (below), one of eighty-eight (compared to the DB's eighteen), worked a freight at Saalfeld in September, 1976.

D.J. Short

Above, A.E. Durrant

Below, Ron Ziel

Above, D. Trevor Rowe

Below, A.E. Durrant

The DR and DB also produced different designs of medium-size 2-6-2 passenger locomotives to succeed the P8 4-6-0s. Built from 1955 to 1959, the DR engines were a much-improved version of two 1941 prototypes; further construction having been prevented by the war. As part of the DR's 1970 computerized renumbering scheme, these 23 10s became Class 35. On July 15, 1964, No. 23 1056 (upper left) hauled a local train of two-axle "Thunderboxes" towards Dresden. No. 35 1055 (lower left) passed Wainsdorf on October 5, 1972; when a brigade of Russian motorized infantry appeared, the photographer hid his cameras! Both the Belpaire-boilered Saxon XII H2 *Rollwagen* and Prussian P8 4-6-0s served the DR until 1972. No. 38 327 (above) pulled a train of vintage compartment stock near Wolkenstein on August 10, 1963. The following year, P8 No. 38 2450 (below) doubleheaded with 2-8-2 No. 22 039 – one of 85 reconstructed Prussian P10s – at Dresden Klötzsche.

1,495 three-cylinder Prussian G12 heavy 2-10-0s were built between 1917 and 1921. With Belpaire boilers and bar frames, they became the first *Einheitslokomotiven,* or standard DRG locomotives. No. 58 1629 (above) rolled a coal train out of Erfurt on July 13, 1964. During 1958-62, the DR modernized fifty-six as Class 58 30, with larger cabs and tenders, new standard boilers, Heinl feedwater heaters and extended bar frames. No. 58 3030 (below) headed a Glauchau-Gera freight at Schmölln on March 28, 1978. Two powerful prewar 2-10-0

designs were the three-cylinder 44 and the two-cylinder 50. The latter, built mostly after 1939 as *Übergangkriegslokomotiven* (ÜK), were much simplified in order to conserve materials; construction of the 44s continued until 1949. No. 44 0567 (upper right), one of 131 oil-fired engines (of the DR's 335), steamed along the *Saalebahn* near Orlamünde on February 1, 1981. No. 50 1002 (lower right), one of a handful of original 50s left in service, crossed the Mulde River at Nossen on April 5, 1982.

Above, A.E. Durrant   Below, Pete Skelton   Opposite, Nils Huxtable

Between 1926 and 1949, 1,989 three-cylinder, 44 Class heavy 2-10-0s were built. In the mist at Etzelbach, No. 44 0196 (above) was Saalfeld-bound on May 31, 1979. "Black engine in the dead of night" was the description given by the photographer of No. 44 0104 (below), about to depart Saalfeld a year later. Enthusiasts had the Russians to thank for the continued use of steam on the *Saalebahn* between Probstzella and Camburg into the 1980s; it was one of those lines de-electrified following the war. The DR built 88 new 50 40 Class Decapods and rebuilt 208 of the 50 Class. Two of the rebuilds (opposite) were at Rogätz (top) on October 2, 1974 and Rosswein (bottom) on July 24, 1980. Both authors took the latter picture, and when the Nossen roundhouse foreman learned they were railroad writers, he requested his engine crews to make smoke as they got into camera range! He also suggested that if this book – at the time in the earliest planning stage – were to sell in the D.D.R. a change of title was required!

Above and below, Pete Skelton   Opposite, Ron Ziel

About half of the 6,576 52 Class *Kriegslokomotiven* erected for the *Wehrmacht* in 1942-45 were kept by both German railways after the War, the rest going to a dozen countries, from Norway to Turkey. At first, the only improvement made to these engines by the DR was the provision of standard Witte smoke deflectors; otherwise, they retained their wartime appearance. No. 52 4908 (left) departed Bad Freienwalde on September 30, 1974. In the 1960s, 200 were reboilered, modified and renumbered in the 8000 series; No. 52 8159 (right) at Genthin was one of these *Rekoloks*. Beginning in 1928, the DRG built 775 86 Class 2-8-2 tanks for light freight and branchline passenger service. No. 86 1501 (below) was arriving at the Crottendorf terminus with the afternoon train from Schlettau on March 3, 1987, in a scene typical of rural Germany during the steam era.

Left and above, Ron Ziel   Below, Pete Skelton

A.E. Durrant

Opposite, Ron Ziel

Among the rare gems on the DR during the 1960s were a few 94.20 Class 0-10-0Ts, a Saxon design of 1908. No. 94 2039 (above), one of 142 constructed, was approaching Dresden with a local freight in 1964. The last one was taken out of service in 1976. An even older design, but erected in huge numbers, was the Prussian T9 2-6-0T, dating from 1893. Many of these engines were originally built for Poland. After the war, some were given as reparations to the PKP, ČSD and SZD, and others were sold to industrial concerns. 2-6-0T No. 91 456 (lower left) worked at Freital Potschappel, near Dresden on August 6, 1963.

A good example of a class that provided reparations disproportionate to the total built was the 89 0 0-6-0T of 1934. Five of the ten went to the PKP and three to the SZD. Of two DR engines left, No. 89 008 (lower right), worked at Dresden, in 1964, three years before being put on display at the *Verkehrsmuseum* in that city. By contrast, modern postwar steam power is represented by Pacific No. 01 1511(opposite, top) with a Leipzig-Saalfeld local at Gera in 1980 and Mikado No. 41 1099 (opposite, bottom), pulling an express near Seehausen in 1974; both engines were rebuilds of prewar DRG standard types.

D. Trevor Rowe

A.E. Durrant

While the 01 5 semi-streamlined Pacifics were perhaps the most famous DR locomotives, there were three other 4-6-2 classes, not counting the two test engines. During the 1930s, 298 03 Class light Pacifics were built; although the DR upgraded 53 out of 74, dieselization caused many to be set aside prematurely. In October, 1974, when No. 03 2207 (upper left) sped along the mainline near Welle, this busy section saw trains at twenty-minute intervals, most still powered by 4-6-2s, 2-8-2s and 2-10-0s. That same month was the 25th anniversary of the D.D.R. and most of the population ignored the celebrations. At Krossen/Elster, an official "25 D.D.R." sign defaced the platform as No. 03 2155 (lower left), began accelerating after a brief station stop. When the photographer commented on the presence of two Soviet Army officers after the station master had granted him permission to take photographs, the man's smile turned to a frown as he said, reassuringly: "*They* have nothing to say about what you do; *I* am the one in charge here!" The DR staff and the authors would have laughed aloud, had they known then that East Germany would barely last until its 40th anniversary! Wagner-deflectored 4-6-2 No. 01 2118 (below), looked much as she did when built, a half-century earlier, as she worked a local mixed freight and passenger train at Weida in 1980.

Three photos, Ron Ziel

Once restrictions on railway photography had been lifted, the D.D.R. could seem almost civilized – if the freedom to take railroad photos was the main criterion. But the visitor lulled into believing meaningful changes had occurred under Erich Honecker did well to remember his shoot-to-kill orders issued to border guards. As a *Stasi* (secret police) agent reminded two British enthusiasts: "Remember, it is easy to *enter* the D.D.R.; it is not so easy to *leave*." The "Soviet Zone" of Germany, a lonely planet of latent Nazism and patent Stalinism, was still a police state subservient to Moscow. But the foreign photographers kept coming – to record the passing of sleek Pacifics such as the immaculate No. 01 2204 (right), topping 50 miles per hour at Oberwellenborn with an *Eilzug* (fast passenger) for Leipzig on July 27, 1980. She and two other classmates had become the most sought-after engines in Europe by this late date. Thirty-five of these 01s were rebuilt into the 01 5 Class; No. 01 0505 (upper right) was providing pre-arranged smoke effects at Oppurg, on the same day. 2-8-2 No. 41 1118 (above), one of 124 (366 were built in the 1930s) on the DR, was also reboilered. Used on both passenger and freight turns until the mid-1980s, they outlasted the Pacifics. This one was speeding through Haldensleben on August 7, 1979.

Two photos above, Nils Huxtable   Below, Ron Ziel

88

Eight 01.5s were originally fitted with Boxpok driving wheels, coned smokebox doors and running-board skirting; all had skyline casing and frontal aprons, creating an impression of power and speed. As "showpiece" engines, they were assigned to cross-border expresses, reaching Bebra, Hamburg and Helmstedt in West Germany. *Kursbuch* (timetable) in hand, the train conductor waited while the driver of No. 01 0510 (left) signed his orders at Saalfeld in May, 1981. Nos. 01 0521 and 0519 (below) occupied adjoining tracks beneath the vast trainshed at Leipzig in 1979. Both trains had come from Saalfeld; one via Jena, the other via Gera. (In the last years of steam, Saalfeld became a mecca for hundreds of foreign photographers, the road bridge at the north end of the station providing a position for high-angle photos like the one forming the rear end-sheet of this book.) The last three of forty-five huge Prussian T20 2-10-2 tanks built in the early 1920s were to be retired on August 1, 1980. Three days before, both authors photographed No. 95 0016 (opposite) near Oberloquitz, working a heavy freight from Saalfeld to Sonneberg. This locomotive was preserved and powered *Plandampf* trains into the 1990s.

Two photos, Pete Skelton   Opposite, Ron Ziel

Above, Ron Ziel

Below, D. Trevor Rowe

D. Trevor Rowe

Ron Ziel

The once-extensive East German narrow-gauge network, comprising both state-owned and private lines, declined during the 1960s and '70s; many were closed, while others were pruned or lost their passenger service. At one time, there had been 550 km. of 75 cm. trackage just in Saxony, where, on the lines that survived, 2-10-2Ts built in the 1950s steamed into the 1990s. No. 99 1783 (upper left), making an early-morning meet at Rabenau in 1980, was one of them. Saxon-Meyer 0-4-4-0T No. 99 551 (lower left), paralleled a standard-gauge line, having crossed under the Karl Marx Stadt (Chemnitz)-Dresden main-

line at Hetzdorf, in August, 1963, with *Rollbockzüge* wagons carrying standard-gauge freight cars. 0-4-4-0Ts, including ex-*Gera-Meuselwitz-Wuitzer Eisenbahn* No. 99 5712 (above left) at Kayna and ex-Saxon IV K No. 99 1606 (above right) at Niederschmiedeberg on the *Pressnitztalbahn,* were familiar sights in this, the most picturesque part of East Germany. Ex-*Nordhausen-Wernigeroder Eisenbahn* No. 99 6001 (below), sole member of a 2-6-2T design by Krupp in 1939, was at Alexisbad in the Harz Mountains on a winter's day in 1987.

Pete Skelton

In the yard at Kyritz on May 29, 1966, former *Kleinbahnen des Kreises Jerichow* 0-8-0T No. 99 4645 (left) headed a mixed train. 1897-built 0-4-4-0T No. 99 5901 (below), restored to its *Nordhausen-Wernigeroder Eisenbahn* identity as No. 11, was easing around a curve near Magdesprüng in March, 1987, following a late winter snowfall. In July, 1980, the authors photographed 2-10-2T No. 99 1791 (lower right) leaving Cranzahl with a morning train to Kurort Oberwiesenthal, as well as 0-4-4-0Ts Nos. 99 1566 and 1562 (upper right), the latter hauling a train of standard-gauge cars on narrow-gauge transporter wagons through the old town of Oschatz. Both of these branches survived into the '90s, although the Oschatz-Mügeln-Kemmlitz line was privatized – and partially dieselized – in 1993. While the downfall of Communism resulted in the creation of a number of new countries, the *Deutsche Demokratische Republik* simply ceased to exist as it was absorbed into West Germany, as did the *Deutsche Reichsbahn,* which became the eastern lines of the new *Deutsche Bahnen.*

Below, Pete Skelton

Above, D. Trevor Rowe

Opposite: top, Nils Huxtable; bottom, Ron Ziel

CZECHOSLOVAKIA

The contrast between venerable and modern steam traction was nowhere more evident than in Czechoslovakia. By the time the last stoker-fitted 2-10-0 rolled off the production line in 1958, the roster of the *Československé Státní Dráhy* – Czechoslovakian State Railways – ranged from an assortment of aging Austrian and Hungarian engines to some of the most technologically-advanced steam power in all of Europe. Out of the dismantled Austro-Hungarian Empire, the states of Bohemia, Moravia and Slovakia were united under the flag of Czechoslovakia. By contrast, the ČSD had considerably more difficulty in establishing *its* identity. It fell heir not only to large portions of the Austro-Hungarian state railway systems and many private operations, but also to a hodge-podge of nearly 200 different classes of locomotives.

From this equivocal legacy, the ČSD salvaged what it could, re-building many engines for the sake of expediency in order to achieve some measure of standardization. Unlike some countries, however, the Czechs did not have to depend on foreign factories to supply their railroad needs. Two former Austrian locomotive builders had been handed over along with the parcel of nationhood; these were soon amalgamated into the ČKD company. From 1920 onward, construction of steam-power was shared between ČKD and the great industrial and weapons manufac-

turer, Škoda.

Apart from 2-6-2 express locomotives and mixed-traffic 2-8-2Ts, the ČSD relied at first on home-produced versions of the ubiquitous Austrian Consolidation. A wide range of types soon followed, however: 4-8-4Ts, 2-10-0s, 2-10-2Ts, 4-6-2s, 2-8-4s and 4-8-2s. What the Great War visited on Austria-Hungary, World War II did to Czechoslovakia. The division of the railways accompanied the carving-up of the country; motive-power and rolling stock were lost to the Nazi colossus and its ally, Hungary. By 1942, Škoda was mass-producing *Kriegsloks* and turning out armaments as never before. But with the end of the War and the re-unification of the Czechoslovak State, ČSD steam really came into its own, despite the imposition of a Communist dictatorship. Czech engineers were quick to apply the latest innovations of French and German steam technology, with the result that all-welded boilers, stokers, Kylchap blastpipes and roller bearings became standard features on everything from 4-8-2s to Decapods.

Railroad photography during Communist times in Czechoslovakia was similar to that experienced in Rumania or Hungary; one never knew what to expect. Several days could be spent freely taking pictures; then suddenly, the police would make arrests – sometimes for no apparent reason. After spending an hour photographing in the yard at Stará Paka, one of the

authors and German enthusiast Rüdiger Weber were returning to their car, when Weber paused to get a photo of an old Mercedes on the street. Apprehension was swift; at headquarters, they were questioned about the photography of antique cars! At Česká Lípa on that same trip, they spent most of the day around the depot and yard, photographing a constant parade of trains, only to be arrested in the early evening– after different policemen had come on duty. When this book was dedicated to the many helpful and sympathetic railway men behind the Iron Curtain, the shed foreman at Rumburk came immediately to mind. When asked by one of the authors for permission to photograph the engine terminal the following morning, his answer was: "Of course, but get here early. The guy who replaces me is a crazy Communist."

To steam enthusiasts, at least, communism in Czechoslovakia must have seemed even crazier than in other East Bloc countries, given the ČSD's policy of retiring modern 2-10-0s, 4-8-2s and 4-8-4Ts – some barely fifteen years old – in favor of home-built diesels. Perhaps the reason for this haste and waste lies in the comment made by one of the great steam designers the Czechs admired so much: André Chapelon. Watching the locomotives he had designed for the French National Railways going for scrap, he remarked, "C'est la mode."

Half a century of steam development separates these two classes. Jutting smokebox, dry steam pipe connecting the domes, cluttered appearance and short, three-axle tender, Austrian-inspired 2-8-0 No. 434.2218 (left) was shoving a snowplow at Vlčí Hora on February 20, 1979. Superpower 2-10-0 No. 556.053 (right) was wreathed in its own steam as it moved a freight out of Rumburk yard on a cool, damp winter evening.

Two photos, Ron Ziel

Opposite: Above, D. Trevor Rowe; Below, C. Gammell

Two photos, A.E. Durrant

In the final years of ČSD steam, the big Mountains of classes 475.1, 498.0 and 498.1 gained fame among photographers, but for elegance, the three-cylinder 387.0 Class Pacifics were without equal. When introduced in 1925, they ushered in a new phase in Czech locomotive construction. With cast steel frames and modifications to the inside valve gear drive, they were highly successful. The prototype, No. 387.001 (above) climbed away from Česká Třebová with an express on May 28, 1960. The last one in the class, No. 387.043 (opposite, above) was at Lužná u. Rakovníka. About half the 387.0s were fitted with double Kylchap exhaust systems. In 1939, Škoda built six heavy (19-ton axle load) Pacifics for Lithuania, but the outbreak of war prevented their delivery, and they became ČSD Class 399.0. They were the only two-cylinder 4-6-2s on the roster. No. 399.003 (right) was at Žalov in 1960. 2-6-2 No. 365.007 (opposite, below) met a 2-8-0 on the Vltava River bridge in Prague on October 12, 1967.

An appreciable number of ancient Austrian steam locomotives were still to be seen in Czechoslovakia in the Spring of 1960, when "Dusty" Durrant managed to photograph a variety of them. Massive diesel deliveries rendered them redundant within just a few years, leaving the more modern ČSD and Škoda engines to close out the age of steam. The four photographs on this spread illustrate as many different wheel arrangements in the twilight of Austrian steam on the ČSD; virtually all were retired before Western photographers began arriving in modest numbers a decade later. A classic Austrian, outside-frame 0-6-0 No. 313.039 (upper far left) was built by the Floridsdorf Works in 1886 for the Kaiser Ferdinand Nordbahn; she was still shunting at Brno seventy-four years later. Austrian

0-8-0s were widespread and long-lived, among them No. 414.013 (upper near left), working a local freight along a Vltava River levee on the outskirts of Prague. With a crewman's bicycle on the running board, 0-10-0 No. 524.089 (lower left) sported an American-looking headlight as she rolled out of Plzeň, renowned for beer, locomotives and armaments. 2-6-0 No. 344.119 (below) led 0-10-0 No. 524.038 on a long freight up the grade out of Česká Třebová. One peculiarity of Austrian locomotives was their double smokebox doors; most steam engines had single doors, hinged on one side. This presented a mild dilemma when it came to affixing the customary big red stars. A combination number plate and star was devised and mounted on top of the smokebox, as modeled by these aging veterans.

Four photos, A. E. Durrant

Following World War II, the *Československé Státní Dráhy* relied on two classes of 2-10-0: the 534.03 Class of 1945, which merely duplicated an existing design of 1923 (with modifications), and the 556.0 Class of 1952. Utilizing the same boiler as the 475.1 as well as a new high-capacity centipede tender, the 556.0s were impressive performers. Capable of hauling 3,000-ton coal trains without assistance, they were observed (by "Dusty" Durrant) triple- and even quadruple-heading out of Puchov – possibly the only other such combination of ten-coupled engines outside China or the former Soviet Union. Imagine the

noise! More than 700 postwar Decapods were built: 200 534.03s between 1945 and 1957 and 510 556.0s during the 1952-57 period. As the fog was lifting near Louny, No. 534.0412 (above) was ready to move its freight when doubleheaded 556.0s – Nos. 0320 and 0218 – received clearance to leave the yard on October 12, 1974. On a cloudy day in 1972, No. 534.0329 (lower right) assembled its freight at Svihov. Among the handful of engines kept for excursions and special events was 0-8-0T No. 422.025 (upper right), lined out in red, with white tires and trim. It participated in a steam festival at Liberec in 1980.

Three photos, Ron Ziel

While the 434 classes of 2-8-0s were the "ugly ducklings" of the ČSD roster, Czech railwaymen were quick to point out that they were of Austrian design, many having been ceded after World War I; others were copies turned out by Czech builders until 1930. Because they were the most numerous of all engines on the roster, many survived until the end of steam. The spunky Consolidations compensated for their esthetic short-comings by noisily accelerating local freights under ample clouds of smoke, as 434.208 (left) was doing at Stará Paka on October 14, 1974. Towards the end of their careers, many 434s were fitted with Giesl ejectors, which did nothing to improve their appearance. Also at Stará Paka, No. 434.2143 (above) was typical of the later version as she shunted the yard. The first ČSD 2-10-0, the 534.0 class, evolved in three stages from an old-fashioned design into a relatively modern-looking secondary freight engine. Minor modifications included a higher-pitched boiler. The one shown below was at Svihov in 1972.

As the standard heavy freight locomotive, the 556.0 Class 2-10-0 operated over the entire ČSD system – and beyond. Prior to the electrification of the Danube River mainline between Bratislava and Budapest, they hauled freight into the Magyar capital; No. 556.0483 (right) was passing Zebegny, Hungary on December 4, 1970. No. 556.0506, peace dove adornments on her smoke deflectors, was the regular cross-border engine between Ceské Velenice and Gmünd, Austria; two halves of a town divided after World War I. A movable section of track would be aligned just long enough to let the 2-10-0 and its train through the Iron Curtain; in the early years of the Cold War, armed frontier guards would accompany enginemen into the West, to ensure their return. For two years following the "Prague Spring" of Alexander Dubček and the Warsaw Pact invasion that smashed it, no red stars were seen on ČSD locomotives, including No. 556.0390 (below), at Bystrice in 1970. A few months later, the symbols of the old order had returned. A gleaming 556.0 (opposite) worked a heavy coal drag at Česká Lípa.

Opposite, Nils Huxtable

Above and below, Ron Ziel

The fireman of No. 556.0501 (left) made adjustments around the smokebox shortly before departing Česká Lípa, the flat-sided Kylchap exhaust housing clearly visible above him. Similar in appearance, though taller and flatter, was the Giesl ejector, as seen on elephant-eared No. 464.016 (below) at Červené Poříčí, working a branchline local on October 27, 1972. This class was the first of a succession of 4-8-4T types on the ČSD. Seventy-six of them were built by Škoda and ČKD between 1933 and 1939. The Hungarian 4-8-0s wandered far afield, and some were taken into ČSD stock, including No. 465.032 (upper right) at Košice in 1961. Engines of different wheel arrangements were sometimes given the same class designation, as illustrated by the two series of 486 power. The 486.0 class, introduced in 1933, were 4-8-2s and the following year, the same components were used for the 486.1 2-8-4 class! Only three were built; ultimately, the 4-8-2 was favored, culminating in the 475.1 and 498 classes developed after the war. No. 486.003 (center right), one of nine prewar 4-8-2s, arrived at Dolny Hričov on August 19, 1958. Berkshire No. 486.103 (lower right) headed a passenger train at Brno two years later.

Two photos, Ron Ziel

Three photos, A.E. Durrant

ČSD tank engines were as fascinating as the tender types. The 423.0 class 2-8-2Ts came in four successive designs, totaling 231 engines over a twenty-four year period. The earlier ones, such as No. 423.041 (below) riding the turntable at Krnov in 1972, had low-pitched boilers and a single casing enclosing the steam and sand domes. Shown at Skalice in 1978, No. 433.031 (lower right) represents the sixty engines upgraded in 1948 with welded boilers. The Austrian 4-6-2 tank was also adopted; the first fifteen, built in 1917, were acquired second-hand. The ČSD ordered 221 more, mostly from Škoda, between 1922 and 1940; No. 354.1120 (above) departed Košice in 1961. The world's most

modern tank locomotive, the three-cylinder 477.0 class 4-8-4T, entered service between 1950 and 1955. The sixty engines embodied the same labor- and fuel-saving devices as their tender engine counterparts, the 498.1 4-8-2s: welded boiler and firebox, stoker, Kylchap exhaust and roller bearings. Smoke deflectors and skyline casing gave them an even more modern look; some were painted lined blue. Preserved No. 477.043 (upper right) came with Trofimoff piston valves and other improvements. One of the 1955 batch, it was photographed at the border station of České Velenice in March, 1993.

Three photos, Nils Huxtable   Above, A.E. Durrant

After 1932, new ČSD tank engine designs concentrated on 4-8-4Ts. Hand-fired 464.018 (above) departed Beroun with a local in 1972. Their heavier predecessors (16-ton axle load compared to 14) were the 2-8-4 suburban tanks; ČKD built twenty-seven between 1927 and 1932. No. 456.002 (below) was at Banská Bystrica in 1960. The three survivors of 147 2-10-2Ts built from 1927 until 1941 for heavy suburban and freight service were still at Rumburk in 1979. The last ČSD tank engine overhauled, No. 524.1110 (right) worked a freight at Valdek on May 29th of that year. A sister engine appears on the front end-sheet of this book.

Above, Ron Ziel   Below, A.E. Durrant

Opposite, Pete Skelton

"Dusty" Durrant describes No. 310.038 (opposite bottom) thus: "The glorious workers march towards a socialist utopia? This train crew seem content to march on their backsides, as they survey their 1897-vintage 0-6-0T at Adamov, June, 1960." Locomotive technology had made considerable progress by the time the 477.0 Class 4-8-4T appeared, more than half a century after the Krauss, Linz 0-6-0T was built. With short side tanks to supplement the rear tank's water capacity and to give greater stability by equalizing weight distribution, No. 477.035 (above) was at Česká Lípa in 1974. Steel sheathing created full-length "false tanks," such as those on No. 477.054 (left) at Skalice; this was a cosmetic improvement. The ČSD's only rack line was the ex-Austrian Reichenbach Gablonz-Tannwalder Eisenbahn. 0-8-2T No. 404.003 (below) pushed its train out of Tanvald; the normal practice on the steepest track sections.

Two photos below, A.E. Durrant

Left and above, Ron Ziel

Popular in Czechoslovakia as elsewhere in Eastern Europe, the 2-6-2 type lasted into the 1960s. The 365.0 Class was the ČSD's first design, dating from 1921. Climbing out of Teplice, No. 365.008 (above) was one of forty such two-cylinder express passenger engines. Former Austrian 2-6-2 No. 354.7145 (below) was heading up the Vltava Valley with a local from Prague. Fitted with a more orthodox smokebox door, No. 354.726 (opposite, above) was about to depart Praha Těšnov. An aging Gölsdorf compound, converted to simple expansion by the ČSD, No. 354.622 (opposite, center) was at Břeclav. The idea behind the connecting pipe, or steam drier, between the domes was to prevent priming. Hungarian 2-6-2s also came to the ČSD; No. 344.404 (opposite, below) remained in former Hungarian territory at Nové Zámky yard on September 18, 1963. The other four photos date from 1960.

Five photos, A.E. Durrant

The various classes of ČSD 4-8-2s were among the most handsome and graceful of locomotives. During the 1947-1950 period, 147 two-cylinder Mountain-types were erected by Škoda. Mixed-traffic engines, they were used mainly in passenger service. Twenty-five additional 4-8-2s were sent to North Korea in 1951, at the height of the Korean War, to relieve the motive-power shortage caused by Allied bombing. One additional 475.1 Class 4-8-2 was presented to the Soviet Union as a gesture of friendship. Among the most modern of European steam locomotives, these 4-8-2s incorporated many of the design innovations of French engineer André Chapelon. As long as mainline passenger trains were handled by steam in Czechoslovakia, the 475.1s, some in blue livery, were often on the head-end. In the gray of December, 1970, a bright red circle having replaced the star during the "Prague Spring" of Alexander Dubček, No. 475.181 (left) at Dynin lacked the high-mounted headlight normally found on these engines. No. 475.183 (below) accelerated out of the yard and onto the mainline at Tábor, while a worker, ignoring both the train and the photographer, painted a spiral stripe on a loudspeaker pole. On May 23, 1972, No. 475.1147 (opposite) stormed away from Zdice, a junction on the Prague-Plzeň main line.

Two photos, Ron Ziel   Opposite, Nils Huxtable

In the aftermath of the Second World War, representatives of several foreign steam classes remained on ČSD rails. There were, of course, the two standard types from the opposing sides in the conflict: the German 52 Class 2-10-0s and, in lesser numbers, the American Army S160 2-8-0s. A total of 300 52 Class were taken into ČSD stock, including some from the Soviet Union. No. 555.3015 (below), posing with its crew at Beroun station in 1972, was an expatriate, first from Germany, then the USSR, as evidenced by the American-style smokebox door applied by the Russians to the 1,500 captured 52s. Compared to the numbers of S-160s which wound up in Hungary and Poland, the seventy-nine which went to Czechoslovakia seem insignificant, but some remained into the 1960s, including No. 456.164 (lower right), heading a local freight in a Spring rainstorm. The original smokebox door had been replaced with a standard Czech one, complete with the obligatory red star. It is interesting to note that while the USSR, Hungary and Czechoslovakia all applied red stars to the fronts of their locomotives (those on ČSD being the most garish), few other engines in Communist countries had them (Just one locomotive of over a hundred seen in Cuba in 1981 had a red star on the cab sides.) Enigmatically, the majority of stars on Bulgarian and Rumanian engines were of bright shining brass, with few red ones evident! Of the thousands of locomotives seen in East Germany, Poland and Yugoslavia none were sporting that most infamous and wide-spread symbol of the Communist system. In 1947, Vulcan Foundry of Great Britain produced a standard 2-8-0 for the United Nations Relief and Rehabilitation Administration (U.N.R.R.A.). Sixty-five of these "Liberation" engines went to Yugoslavia, thirty to Poland and fifteen to Czechoslovakia. With a nineteen-ton axle load, they were the heaviest of the wartime 2-8-0s, and the ČSD employed them partly on banking duties out of Česká Třebová. In the lead on this occasion, No. 459.008 (right) was doubleheading with Austrian 2-8-0 No. 434.248 on the climb through Šemanín in 1961. Both the victors and the vanquished made contributions to the steam stock of most Central and East European railroads; the ČSD was no exception.

Below, Nils Huxtable

Above and below, A.E. Durrant

Above, Ron Ziel

A lenghtened variation of the 387.0 Class Pacific, the prewar 4-8-2s were better-suited to hauling increasingly heavy passenger trains. In turn, the forty-two three-cylinder 498.0 Class Mountains built in 1946 were a development of the 486.0 4-8-2, but with refinements, including a boiler and firebox of mainly welded construction, steel girder-type frames and a variable axle load. These engines were contemporaries of the light-weight, two-cylinder 475.1s. Altogether, over 200 4-8-2s were built for the ČSD – more than for all the other railways in Europe combined. During the winter of 1970-71, No. 498.007 (above) passed through Bystrice, and No. 498.040 (upper left) was at Tábor. According to "Dusty" Durrant, "the finest express

Opposite: Top, Basil Roberts; Bottom, Nils Huxtable

locomotives in Eastern Europe" were the fifteen 498.1s, with roller bearings throughout and boiler improvements, as well as smaller German-style smoke deflectors. Built by Škoda during 1954-55, they were the final express passenger engine design. No. 498.101(lower left) scorched the ballast at Zdice with a Prague-Plzeň express in 1972; a year before withdrawal. A pair of these engines, led by No. 498.109 (below) double-headed the *Balt-Orient Express* between Brno and Bratislava in 1963. Riding behind just *one* 498.1 was perhaps the ultimate in East European steam travel; to quote one British enthusiast, a 498.1 produced "powerful, rasping, three-cylinder noises and fire-work displays."

Below, A.E. Durrant

Above and below, Werner Reber

Unlike other East European rail systems, the ČSD had few narrow gauge lines. Mostly private industrial concerns, all but a handful were dieselized by the early 1960s. Some forestry lines still ran steam, however: 0-8-0T No. 7 (upper left) was at Valašsko and No. U45.903 (lower left) at Lieskova; both in June, 1973. The letter "U" signified *Úzkorozchodné* (narrow gauge) and preceded the class designation of all ČSD narrow-gauge engines. A robust little *lok* (above) worked a long string of four-wheel dumpcars upgrade in Moravia on March 18, 1977. Beer-lovers will appreciate heavy 0-6-0T No. 1842 (right), named *Prazdroj* after the Plzeň brewery where the standard-gauge shunter worked on August 3, 1960.

Above, Pascal Pontremoli   Below, D. Trevor Rowe

YUGOSLAVIA

Few countries boasted a more varied collection of steam locomotives than Yugoslavia. While other railways in Eastern Europe had achieved a level of standardization by the 1960s, the *Zajednica Jugoslovenskih Železnica* – The Community of Yugoslav Railways (JŽ) – was still operating its branchlines and secondary services with a motley array of absorbed steam-power. Aging former Austrian freight engines could be found barking their way through the mountains of Slovenia, while Serbian and former Hungarian 2-6-2s wheeled local passenger trains and an occasional express out of Belgrade and Zagreb.

Railroads came late to the states comprising Yugoslavia, the Turks not laying the first rails in the Balkans until 1872. The conquering Austrians used the line for military purposes; soon the Serbian State Railway's tracks to Bulgaria and Turkey became the main route from Central Europe to Istanbul. Thereafter, the rail network developed slowly, with the construction of many narrow-gauge feeder lines, as well as the standard-gauge main routes. German and Austrian locomotives dominated the motive-power rosters until World War I, when several classes of American engines of both gauges arrived; European builders, all inundated with orders from their own governments, were unable to fulfill any more contracts. The Great War destroyed the old order in Europe, playing havoc with the boundaries of nations and railways alike. Yugoslavia – a name without a country – emerged from the ruins of the Austro-Hungarian Empire, a grouping of warring factions forced into a fragile union. A further obstacle was the disparity of the railways; Serbian and former Empire lines were standard-gauge, while lines further south were mostly 76 cm. and meter-gauge.

Between the wars the JŽ (originally JDŽ) began to modernize its ragtag locomotive roster with three classes: 4-6-2 for passenger service, 2-8-2 for general work and a three-cylinder 2-10-0 for heavy freight haulage. All were German-built, with interchangeable parts, patterned to some extent after recently-introduced *Reichsbahn* engines. Suffering more than its share of vicissitudes in World War II, Yugoslavia became a Communist dictatorship under the clenched fist of Josef Broz Tito, whose uncompromising rule kept the feuding nationalities under control. On the JŽ, the motive-power situation was chaotic, small groups of engines from seven countries being assimilated.

With its crazy assortment of steam engines, the JŽ was a prime target for dieselization to complement its expanding electrification. In Yugoslavia, as well as other Eastern European countries, it was not uncommon to see half-century-old steam engines belching coal smoke onto glistening new copper catenary after the costs of electrifying a line left no money to purchase expensive foreign-built electric locomotives! By 1970, steam was already being phased out, and the standard Decapods, Pacifics and Mikados were retired even before most of the former Austrian and German classes were withdrawn. For the locomotives which survived into the 1980s – the ex-DR 2-10-0s, the U.S. Army 0-6-0Ts, the MÁV-designed 4-8-0s, 2-6-2s and 2-6-2Ts and the Serbian 2-6-2s and 2-6-0s – it was a clear case of strength in numbers.

The attitude of the Yugoslavs – both Milicja and citizenry – made the pursuit of steam a challenging and often futile exercise. Suffice it to say that only in Yugoslavia could the holders of a rare photographic permit be arrested and detained for having been issued

the required authorization! Such were the grounds for the interrogation of the authors in 1980, at the hands of a former Titoist partisan commander, in whose office were displayed bayonets and other war memorabilia – an encounter that can only be described as chilling. Although one of the authors spent just 3% of his red star photography time in Serbia, five of his fifteen arrests occurred there. Given the tensions prevailing in *peacetime,* one can better appreciate the causes of the warfare following the disintegration of Yugoslavia.

Ironically, just before the break-up of the country, a steam tourist service was introduced in Slovenia, using a trio of mainline locomotives, with photo run-pasts! Even so, the idea of freely photographing steam anywhere in the former Yugoslavia was hard to reconcile with co-author Huxtable's memory of being confronted by a truckload of soldiers fifteen years previously and thrown into a cell for doing exactly the same thing! That was Slovenia, about to win its independence from Belgrade – with a minimum of bloodshed. Other breakaway states in Yugoslavia would not be so fortunate.

Opposite. Ron Ziel

Above, A. E. Durrant

Hungarian locomotives were active on the Yugoslav railroads right into the final days of steam. A MÁV 375 Class 2-6-2T, No. 51-142 (opposite), powered a typical two-car branchline local beneath the gray winter Croatian sky at Stubličke Toplice, on February 9, 1979. The celebrated Hungarian 424 Class 4-8-0, bereft of the large smoke deflectors fitted to later members of the class, was not nearly as impressive as the "elephant eared" JŽ version shown on page 7. Thirteen of them remained in Yugoslavia after World War II and were so well-liked that forty-nine more were ordered from Hungary. No. 11-031 (above) blasted upgrade with a Split to Zagreb train at Kastel Stari, Croatia on September 14, 1959.

The JŽ rostered a variety of tank engine classes, mostly of Austro-Hungarian and German origin and later, the World War II United States Army Transportation Corps 0-6-0Ts. With their chunky, bullish appearance, the USATC shunters were nicknamed "Buffaloes" by Yugoslav railwaymen, such as the friendly crew posing with No. 62-085 (above), taking a break from their night shift in the yard at Mladenovač, Serbia on July 3, 1980. No. 62-049 (upper right), rusty and grimy and nearing the end of her career, switched a coal car at Lapovo, in Croatia. The JŽ was so pleased with the 106 American tank engines it had received that

between 1956 and 1959, twenty-three locomotives of the same design were built at Slavonski Brod, incorporating plate instead of bar frames. Formerly an Austrian 93 Class, 2-8-2T No. 53-015 (below) easily handled a local passenger accomodation of five four-wheel cars through the Croatian farmland at Grabno in 1974. In 1922, Henschel outshopped fifty light 0-6-0Ts, which were an updating of a proven Serbian Railways design. No. 61-044 (lower right) shunted the yard at Creveni Krst, Serbia in low evening sunlight on October 23, 1968.

Above and below, Ron Ziel   Opposite (top), Nils Huxtable; (bottom), C. Gammell

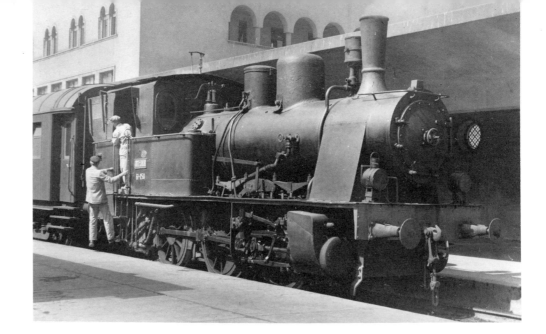

Yugoslav tank engines in the 1950s — a time when very few photographs were being made of steam beneath the red star! Among the last of the 1922 0-6-0Ts, No. 61-050 (opposite, top) shunted at Skopje, the Macedonian capital's Moorish-style station in September, 1953. At the other end of the country, former Hungarian State Railways 2-6-2T No. 17-018 (opposite, center) had been a MÁV class 342, eighty-nine of which were built during World War I. Most were absorbed by the railways of the Kingdom of the Serbs, Croats and Slovenes (the original name for Yugoslavia) immediately following the war. Photographed at Sežana, a Slovenian station on the Italian border, No. 17-018 was typically Balkan in appearance in this October, 1952 pose, with Brotan boiler, tall stack and Pecz-Rejto water purifier in front of the sand dome. Hungary's compact little branchline 2-4-2T, class 22 (later class 275), was first supplied to Yugoslavia in 1922. The shops at Slavonski Brod built a further twenty-two in 1939-1941, including No. 16-029 (opposite, bottom), seen at Sombor, Serbia in 1952. 0-6-0 tender engines of Hungarian lineage could also be found on JŽ rails. A small outside-frame version, No. 125-043 (above), was working the yard at Sišak, Croatia in September, 1959; the crew unaware they were being photographed. A larger, inside-frame Magyar 0-6-0, No. 120.019 (below), her service life nearly over in 1980, was a minehead switcher at Resavica.

Four photos, A. E. Durrant   Below, Ron Ziel

131

Among the less numerous of JŽ types was the ex-Prussian G-12 class, a big, chunky Decapod. No. 36-048 (left) peddled through the yard at Nova Gorica, Slovenia in May, 1971. With the driver smiling from the cab of fierce-looking Austrian veteran 2-10-0 No.29-022 (lower left), the train moved slowly upgrade from Židani Most, through the way station at Radeče, Slovenia in 1959. Ten of these locomotives arrived new from Austria after the First World War, with twenty-seven (including this one) added second-hand in 1946. Along with the Hungarian 424 class 4-8-0s, which arrived following World War II, a contemporary Austrian Twelve-wheeler also found a new home on the JŽ in the 1940s. Just five of them (of forty built in 1923-1928) were ceded to Yugoslavia; No. 10.001 (right) sped through Radeče with a Zagreb-bound express. Prussian G-10 0-10-0s wandered over much of Eastern Europe, and the JŽ rostered its share of them. Photographer Durrant, commenting on the picture of former G 10 No. 35-163 (below), wrote: "The lighting pole was a photographic nuisance, perhaps balanced by the sturdy peasant woman marching determinedly about her own business" at Sunja, Croatia in 1959.

Upper left, Nils Huxtable
Three photos, A. E. Durrant

Above and below, A. E. Durrant

Above and below, D. Trevor Rowe

While America boasted the largest locomotives in the world, the smaller 2-8-0 was the most common freight engine. Most East European railroads, however, favored the larger and more powerful 2-10-0 as standard freighthauler, the Consolidation being employed on less-demanding duties. On the JŽ, four 2-8-0 classes survived in modest numbers until dieselization. At the head-end of a passenger train at Zdani Most, Slovenia in 1963, No. 25-024 (lower left) was one of thirty-four 2-8-0s which came from Austria following both World Wars. The wide spacing of the wheels on No. 26-060 (upper left), at Sišak in 1959, was to spread the weight when crossing light bridges. One hundred of these engines were built for the Serbian Railways by the Germans in 1923. The UNRRA sent thirty-five U.S. Army 2-8-0s, with more being acquired from Italy, including No. 37-043 (above), wheeling a crowded train out of Belgrade on September 1, 1961. Still lettered "UNRRA", Nos. 38-047 and 38-029 (below) at Novi Beograd in 1964, were two of the sixty-five Vulcan Liberation-type Consolidations also supplied by the United Nations after World War II.

As in most of the rest of Eastern Europe, the popularity of the 2-6-2 – both tender and tank versions – in Yugoslavia was evident right up until the end of steam operations. The *Žaljednica Jugoslovenskih Železnica* steam locomotive which will be remembered the longest is surely the 01 class 2-6-2, a simple four-cylinder design which was versatile, fast and powerful. As World War I reparations, 126 were delivered to the Serbian, Croatian & Slovenian Railways, where they became the most widespread of medium passenger power. Even in July, 1980, with the steam era drawing to a close, these Prairie-types, such as shining, red-trimmed No. 01-092 (left) at Brzan, could be found on many local passenger moves. A decade earlier, on November 29, 1970, while giving two attractive local college girls a ride in his rented Volkswagen, the photographer came upon the engine terminal at Lapovo, teeming with locomotives in the low afternoon sunlight. Photographing an 01, he was promptly pounced upon by railwaymen and the police, who marched him towards the station. The entire roundhouse staff of about twenty men surrounded the group, passing around what was probably the first American passport they had ever seen and momentarily forgetting the perpetrator who, excusing himself, elbowed his way through the crowd and photographed No. 01-101 (lower left), with No. 33-126 in the background, before he was re-apprehended. With one of the hitch-hikers interpreting, the interrogation so fascinated the inquisitors that they forgot all about the film! She later told the photographer that he could always expect such a furor, since the police chief had telephoned his superiors to report the arresting of a potential spy, thereby impressing them with his vigilance. On a less exciting Autumn day in Rogatec, Slovenia, four years later, two ex-MÁV engines, 2-6-2T No. 51-053 and 2-6-2 No. 22-076 (below), double-headed a freight, their red-trimmed flanks glistening in the sunlight.

Three photos, Ron Ziel

On a bright Serbian summer morning in 1980, co-author Huxtable, having just photographed 2-6-2 No. 01-088 (below) at Kragujevac, waves to the engine crew. A 2-6-2 of the MÁV 324 class was No. 22-069 (above), working a local between Zadok and Podsused Stajaliśte, Croatia on October 25, 1974, the characteristic hump of the Brotan boiler visible directly ahead of the cab. After the First World War, a total of sixty compound Mallet locomotives of three different wheel arrangements (2-4-4-0, 0-6-6-0, 2-6-6-0) was turned over to Yugoslavia by the Hungarians. The largest of the three classes consisted of thirty-six 2-6-6-0s, some of which survived until the mid-1960s as the last mainline Mallets in Europe. No. 32-026 (upper right) rolled downgrade through Kastel Stari on September 14, 1959, and No. 32-022 (lower right) basked in the afternoon sunshine at Perkovic in 1957; both in Croatia.

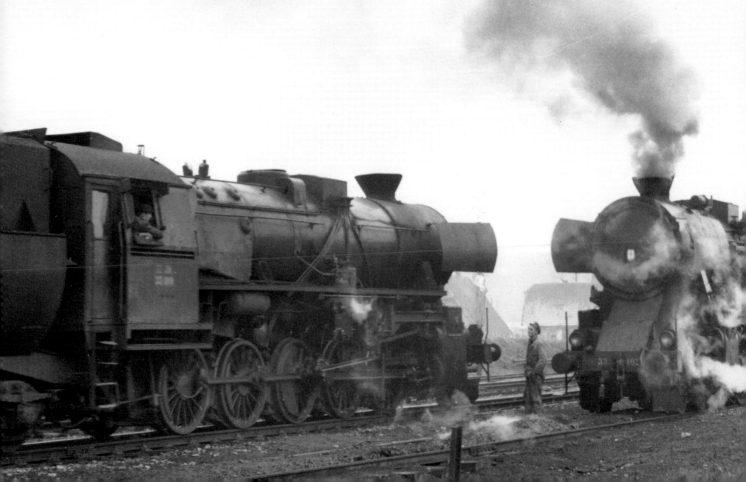

Three photos, Ron Ziel

The ubiquitous German 52 Class 2-10-0s, 346 of which came to the JŽ after World War II, some via the USSR, were active right into the 1980s. The 52s inherited by the Yugoslavs had few modifications; even at the end of the steam era, they looked essentially as built. On the morning of July 5, 1980 the authors discovered a *Kriegslok* hauling – of all things – a Russian-built T-34 tank, the most effective of Second World War Soviet armor. In a scene reminiscent of the wartime era nearly forty years previously, when captured T-34s were taken from the frontlines behind German Army 52s, Decapod No. 33-068 (upper left) plied a branch near Sedlare. Nos. 33-109 and 33-102 (lower left) met at Donji Potok, Bosnia, in the morning mist on November 28, 1970. While railroad photography was suspect in most Communist countries, picture-taking at bridges and tunnels was especially frowned upon. Continuing in pursuit of No. 33-109, the photographer encountered her coming out of a tunnel near Tinja (above) and crossing two bridges – a combination guaranteed to cause trouble. As the 2-10-0 rolled by, the engineer leaned out of the cab, scowled and gave the photographer the standard manacled wrists gesture. Police waiting down the road took the suspect to where the 33-109 was simmering alongside their headquarters, the enginemen crossing their wrists again and grinning as the photographer was led inside. This incident was unfolding just a short time after a state visit to Yugoslavia by then American President Richard M. Nixon. With the captive's 4" x 5" camera and film holders on his desk, the police chief seemed uncertain as to what should be done, once he had made the customary telephone calls to his superiors. Seizing on the indecision of the moment, the photographer pointed to the official portrait of a frowning Marshal Tito hanging on the soot-encrusted wall and extending his right hand, pronounced: "Tito, Nixon, friends; you, me, friends!" "Da, DA", exclaimed the chief, vigorously shaking the suspect's hand, "friends, FRIENDS!" Handing over the camera and holders, the chief escorted the photographer to his car.

141

There were additional Austrian locomotive classes, in lesser numbers, ceded to the JŽ, three of which are shown here. Having first gone to Italy and later Yugoslavia, 2-6-2 No. 106-012 (above) was a superheated compound engine working at Doboj Novi, Bosnia on September 11, 1957. An interesting double-header combination, but pulling a rather anemic train, was 4-6-0 No. 03-002 (below), leading 2-10-0 No. 29-016 out of Zidani Most,

Slovenia, six years later. Another Decapod, No. 145-001 (upper right), was built for the *Südbahn* (Southern Railway) of Austria in 1912. The retreating *Wehrmacht* left it behind in 1944; it is seen working under catenary at Divača, Slovenia in 1955. One of the three standard classes developed in 1929-1930 was the handsome 06 Mikado; No. 06-009 (lower right) headed a fast freight at Zdani Most on September 10, 1963.

Four photos, A. E. Durrant

Opposite, C. Gammell

Above and below, D. Trevor Rowe

The 05 class Pacifics, contemporaries of the 06 2-8-2s, were retired early, with few photographs of them available. A few were still active into the late 1960s, including the trim 4-6-2 (opposite) heading the *Direct Orient Express* away from Creveni Krst, Serbia in 1968. Yugoslavia boasted the most extensive narrow-gauge system in Europe into the Communist era, but by the 1960s it was being rapidly abandoned or converted to standard-gauge. Among the closures was the *Gradska Željeznica,* whose 1947 Polish-built

0-4-0T No. 1121-04 (above) was about to depart from Zagreb, Croatia on September 15, 1958. Narrow-gauge track was often undulating and poorly maintained, so some of the lines in Bosnia-Herzegovina used locomotives with the semi-articulated Klose system of machinery and suspension, enabling them to negotiate the poor track. No. 189-022 (below) was an 0-6-2T of the Klose type, shown at Srnetica in 1961 with an American-built UNRRA 0-8-0 in the background.

Among the most handsome of standard-gauge tank engines on the JŽ was the 17 class 2-6-2T. No. 17-042 (opposite, bottom) was coupled to a local passenger train at Subotica, Vojvodina on June 21, 1974. The 83 class 0-8-2 was one of the best and most prolific of 76 cm. gauge locomotives, with 187 built in various sub-classes and modified over a forty-six-year period, ending in 1949. No. 83-045 (opposite, top) was at Koplare and No. 83-035 (above) rested at twilight at Mladenovac – both in Serbia – in 1980. Considered among the most advanced of 76 cm.-gauge engines, the versatile 85 class 2-8-2, with its high-capacity tender, had wide availability. No. 85-032 (below) was one of thirty-five built in Hungary in 1930, with a further ten supplied by Slavonski Brod a decade later. It is shown with 83-138 at Hum, Bosnia in 1961.

Opposite, Nils Huxtable   Above, Ron Ziel   Below, D. Trevor Rowe

So little remains of the once-thriving JŽ narrow-gauge, it is difficult now to appreciate the amazing variety of steam-power that once worked the four different gauges. Gone are the meter-gauge 0-6-2Ts, such as 1898-vintage Krauss No. 42 (above) being serviced at Osijek, Croatia in May, 1955, and her eight-, ten- and twelve-coupled sisters of the Slavonian Drava Valley Railway. Vanished too are the *Feldbahn* engines of the 60 cm. Skopje-Lake Ochrid line, along whose curving mountain trackage No. 99-4-101 (upper right) was taking water at Strazara, Macedonia in 1961. Centered in Belgrade, the 76 cm. mainline of Europe once featured spirals, tunnels and rack sections through the mountains, express trains with dining cars and a profusion of 0-8-2s, 2-8-2s, 2-6-6-0

Mallets and 0-6-4 rack tanks for hauling passengers and freight to Sarajevo, Titograd, Ploce and Dubrovnik. In 1970, this famous system was replaced by a new standard-gauge line. Running on very light rail, meter-gauge 0-8-0T No. 56 (below) trundled through the yard at Orahovica, Croatia on May 15, 1964. This engine and her eight sisters, built by Krauss for the SDV Railway during the decade preceding the First World War, were to power the last trains to run on the meter-gauge lines at the time of their abandonment. Ambling into Paračin, Serbia with a 76 cm.-gauge train of tiny coaches was 0-6-2T No. 72-014 (lower right) in August, 1958.

Upper right and below, D. Trevor Rowe   Lower right and above, A. E. Durrant

Narrow-gauge railroad operations have a fascination all their own. The combination of slim track gauge, diminutive size of the equipment, informal operations and often remote and scenic landscapes piques one's interest and curiosity; even though most narrow-gauge operations have now succumbed, the mystique endures. In the golden age of the narrow-gauge, Yugoslavia offered a variety of all of the aforementioned unmatched anywhere else in the world. 0-4-4-0T No. 90.006 (above), at Cuprija, Serbia in 1961, was the most basic of compound engines. A 76

cm. 2-8-0, No. 84-004 (below), worked at Sarajevo in 1958, forty-three years and two World Wars after having been outshopped by the American Locomotive Company in 1915. Unusually handsome for an outside-frame engine, No. 73-001 (upper right) worked a well-patronized local train at Bosanski Brod, Bosnia on May 16, 1964. Four-cylinder rack locomotive No. 97-011 (lower right) awaited her next run at Konjic, Bosnia in 1958; tragically, thirty-five years later, this was to become a major battleground of the post-Communist ethnic war.

Three photos, D. Trevor Rowe

Below, A. E. Durrant

150

Above, Frank Quin, Ziel collection

Following World War II, the UNRRA ordered a fleet of 0-8-0s from Davenport and Vulcan in the USA. (Vulcan of Great Britain built the standard-gauge UNRRA engines.) Thirty-four of them were produced for the Bosnian 76 cm. lines. Nos. 18 and 19 (above) were loaded on flatcars in America, en route to the docks. Still lettered UNRRA, No. 17 (below) was leaving Prijedor in 1961. Virtually the entire narrow-gauge system was to follow standard-gauge JŽ steam into oblivion over the next quarter-century; eventually most of the warring states which comprised Yugoslavia disintegrated into chaos and bloodshed.

Below, D. Trevor Rowe

ALBANIA

Above, Uwe Bergmann, Florian Schmidt collection

During the Cold War, no country was more isolated from the rest of the world than Albania. Bordered on the north and east by Yugoslavia, the south by Greece and the west by the Adriatic Sea, its frontiers were tightly sealed and its contacts with the outside world – including other Communist states – few and totally lacking in cultural and other exchanges. Its single railway line did not begin operating until 1947, and little was known of its steam traction, except that it had acquired some Polish tank engines of the Tkt-48 type and possibly a few Okl-27s before those. The authors had heard that some photographs of Albanian steam were available, but if indeed any exist, they failed to materialize, except for one Polish 2-8-2T. Once the Communists were out and the country opened up in 1990, it was too late for operating steam.

One group of Germans did get into Albania in 1985 and at the port city of Durrës, they found a solitary, decrepit Tkt-48, No. 02 (above), wheezing around the yard. Visitors after the fall of Communism saw Czechoslovakian diesels at work, and the surviving green-liveried steam locomotives were mere derelict hulks (below), scattered about in varying stages of decay.

Below, P. R. Bowen

J.B. Snell

BULGARIA

Bulgaria's steam locomotives were as rugged as the country they served. Against the tortuous mountain grades, the Bulgarian State Railways (BDZ) pitted some of the toughest steamers ever built on the European continent. The BDZ went in for big power in a big way, rejecting Mallets in favor of massive three-cylinder 2-12-4 tank engines which were heavier and carried more coal and water than the largest British tender locomotives! The Bulgarians also opted for an impressive and successful modern 4-10-0, a wheel arrangement never popular with other railroads and completely rejected before 1900. Beefy wartime German Decapods, through sheer numbers the most representative BDZ type, made up more than a third of the steam roster. Decked out in green paint, with red frames and wheels, Bulgarian steam left more than a fleeting impression.

Bulgaria's basic railway network was not completed until the late nineteenth century. Finding places of sufficient population density to warrant rail service was almost as difficult as cutting through the mountain ranges to get to them. Thus, the earliest lines in Bulgaria were built, not so much to connect the towns they passed through as to establish international routes between Central Europe and Istanbul.

By 1888, when the BDZ was established, lines had been built from the Danube River to the Black Sea and to Plovdiv. In the same year, a new line from Plovdiv to Sofia and the Serbian border was opened, and over those tracks ran the first through *Orient Express* of 1889.

As railroads branched out to tap Bulgaria's mineral and agricultural wealth, existing six and eight-coupled locomotives, which had pulled the BDZ's trains into the Twentieth Century, were supplemented by scores of mountain-mauling 0-10-0 compounds, many of which survived to the end of steam as simple engines. These and their contemporaries kept the railroads running until the arrival of more advanced power.

The BDZ's modernization plans of the 1930s called for larger and more powerful designs, built to *Reichsbahn* standards in Germany, Poland and Switzerland. The final phase of steam construction coincided with the Second World War, as the interest of the BDZ in three-cylinder power continued unabated until 1943. Germany continued to supply big, modern locomotives into World War II, but further orders were cancelled by pressure on the factories to increase production of standard DR engines. Meanwhile, a few foreign classes were brought to the BDZ during the war years, including ex-Prussian 2-10-0s loaned by the DR, a few more Decapods intended for Turkey and a small class of

Czech 2-8-2s originally meant for China. There followed the omnipresent German wartime Austerity 2-10-0s.

Unlike neighboring Rumania and Yugoslavia, Bulgaria had but a few narrow-gauge lines, including a pair of *Feldbahn* 60 cm. branches, operated by diminutive tank engines. Two 76 cm. lines, centered on Cervenbreg and Septemvri, comprised the remaining BDZ narrow-gauge operations. Considering the mountainous terrain, with its relatively sparse population, it seems odd that more of the economically and operationally inexpensive narrow-gauge lines were not built.

As in the remainder of Communist East Europe, Bulgaria relied heavily on its railways as the most important means of transport. In general, the attitude towards the photography of locomotives was more reasonable than that of other Eastern Bloc countries. More isolated than other railway systems, the BDZ was not well-chronicled. These factors, plus the standardization, reliability and efficiency of Bulgaria's

big, modern steam locomotives, seemingly destined them to endure longer than any other Warsaw Pact steam roster, but sadly, that was not to be. The policy of the BDZ was to dieselize the mountain trackage early on and to progressively electrify. The diesels were then quickly transferred to the remaining pockets of steam operation. Last of the Eastern Bloc countries to build a national railroad system, Bulgaria became, in 1980, the first to rid itself of regular service steam-traction.

The twenty-two 4-10-0 three-cylinder engines ordered by BDZ during World War II (ten from Henschel, 1940-41, seven from Borsig and five from Skoda in 1943), were to be the only examples of that wheel arrangement built in the 20th Century. They excelled as fast freight haulers, but became early victims of dieselization; all were retired by 1970. One of the last, No. 11.03 (opposite), backed through the yard at Vakarel in June, 1968. At Turnovo it was possible to get unusual high-angle photos of the bridge over the Yantra River from a steep hillside. On May 10, 1964, 0-10-0 No. 28.49 and 2-10-0 No. 16.74 (below), double-headed a mixed freight across the picturesque span.

D. Trevor Rowe

While the BDZ, like most Eastern European rail systems, rostered a preponderence of 2-10-0s, it also had some fine classes of rather handsome passenger power – all of German design, but with very American-appearing front-ends, complete with big headlights and horizontal-bar pilots. In 1931, the Germans built the first truly modern locomotives for the BDZ: large 2-8-2s for passenger service, followed by additional examples from Poland in 1935. One of the latter, No. 01.16 (upper left), sped a heavy passenger train near the capital, Sofia, on May 17, 1965. Despite the demands of wartime production for the DR, Henschel managed to erect a dozen superb three-cylinder 4-8-2s for the BDZ in 1942. Handsome, smooth-riding and fast, they were very popular with their engine crews; perhaps the finest locomotives ever to burnish BDZ rails. The prototype, No. 03.01 (lower left), rolled into Gorna Orjahovitsa with a train from Varna on May 15, 1961. Seen the same month,

Pacific No. 05.02 (below), was one of just five three-cylinder passenger engines with six-coupled driving wheels. As such, they were the only exclusively express steam locomotives ever ordered by the BDZ. This one was caught taking water at Orizovo, as the photographer was riding through on another train. The very nature of the topography and service demands in Bulgaria precluded the need for high-speed engines such as the 05s, requiring instead, trouble-free performance under conditions of low maintenance. Such relatively uncomplicated accessories as stokers were ruled out even on the largest power in favor of dual-firing, a mixture of coal and oil being used in accordance with the rate of steaming required; the more oil added, the greater volume of steam produced. Straightforward and uncomplicated, with no ostentation, were the traits of BDZ steam traction.

Upper left, D. Trevor Rowe   Lower left and below, A. E. Durrant

The BDZ's quest for locomotives of great power began in 1910, with the delivery of the first 2-8-0s designed by Maffei, featuring four compound cylinders – two enormous low-pressure ones outside the frame and high-pressure ones inside. The design was enlarged to a 2-10-0, and during the 1913-1917 period, seventy were built; they were to be the largest and most powerful locomotives on the system, prior to the modernization program of the 1930s. Already forty-four years old, No. 19.43 (left), her large high-mounted cylinders canted downward, crossed the Yantra River at Turnovo, in 1961. After a major overhaul, locomotives were customarily broken in by running around the nearby yards and even hauling local trains, prior to having final adjustments and being painted. Such was the case with No. 19.02 (below), shown fresh out of the Sofia works and appearing incomplete. The absence of the shielding beneath the smokebox front clearly shows the inside high-pressure cylinders, and both photos reveal the counterbalances on the third driving-wheels to be mismatches of those on the other wheels, a common compensation for the thrust of the inside pistons, which also powered the center axle. The *Reichsbahn* 50-class Decapods which came to the BDZ – approximately fifty in number – were operated mostly in the central region. Accelerating out of Plovdiv, No. 14.24 (upper right) proved the appeal of Bulgarian steam beneath the *gold* star, as evidenced by the winged wheel and star emblem of the BDZ on the smokebox door. Not all Bulgarian engines were painted green; 2-12-4T No. 46.02 (lower right), modeled a more conservative black livery (with the usual red trim and gold star) at Sofia, in 1967.

Above and below, A. E. Durrant

Upper right, Nils Huxtable   Lower right, B. Roberts

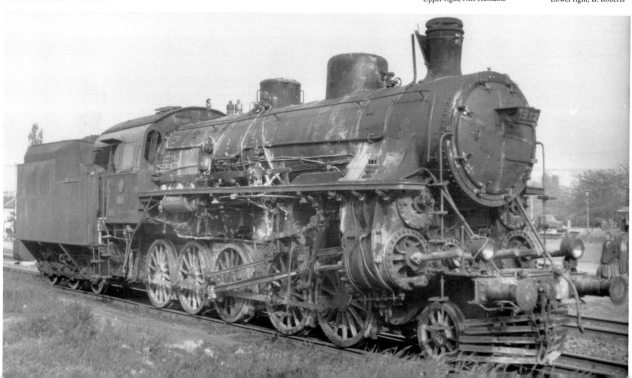

Americans have always assumed that their steam locomotives were the world's largest and most powerful. Not so in the category of non-articulated tank engines; the biggest mainline U.S. examples having been six-coupled, while eight- and ten-coupled classes were common in Europe. But nowhere, except Bulgaria, was it possible to find a whole fleet with a wheel-arrangement as audacious as the 2-12-4T! The initial dozen were two-cylinder engines, built by Cegielski of Poland in 1931, followed by eight three-cylinder updates by Schwartzkopf in 1943. They were employed mainly in the short-run hauling of coal and mineral trains into Sofia from nearby mountain mines.

The earlier two-cylinder series, such as No. 46.12 (below), pulling empty coal cars upgrade at Pernik Loop on May 5, 1964, boasted statistics worthy of heavy American tender engines, weighing 149 tons and exerting tractive effort of more than 70,000 pounds. Its exhaust reverbrating through Gorna Banya in 1961, three-cylinder No. 46.19 (opposite) weighed 155 tons; by comparison, a typical American 4-8-2 weighed 170 tons, but produced only about 60,000 pounds tractive effort. During the final months of BDZ steam, with fewer than twenty remaining active locomotives, 2-6-2T No. 35.44 (above), built by Schwartzkopf in 1921, switched Levski yard on July 9, 1980.

Below, D. Trevor Rowe

Above, Ron Ziel

Opposite, A. E. Durrant

Among the earliest types of locomotive to usher in the modernization of the Bulgarian State Railways during the 1930s was a typically German simple Decapod for both passenger and freight duties. No. 10.12 (upper left), did a passenger turn near Sofia in May, 1965, and No. 10.15 (above) assisted 2-12-4T No. 46.19 on a heavy freight leaving Sofia four years earlier. The three-cylinder Mikados of the mid-1930s were clean-lined and modern; No. 02.03 (below), was being checked by her crew prior to departing with a passenger train from Popovitza in 1965. A BDZ locomotive fresh from a complete overhaul at the Sofia Shops was a sight to behold! In its livery of green, red, white and black with polished brass trim, a former German 52-class Decapod (lower left), looked more like a plastic model as it was being fired up, just hours ex-works, in 1967.

Upper left and below, D. Trevor Rowe   Lower left, B. Roberts   Above, A. E. Durrant

The Prussian T-16 (DR 94-class) 0-10-0T was a heavy shunter, more than 1,200 having been built between 1913 and 1924. Those which got to Bulgaria saw service until late in the steam era, including No. 50.05 (upper left) at Sofia on July 26, 1977. The 76 cm. narrow-gauge lines utilized some large 2-10-2T locomotives. Built by Chrzanów in 1940, No. 606.76 (lower left) was heading into Orjahovo, and No. 615.76 (below) was at the engine terminal in Cervenbreg; both in 1974. 0-6-2T No. 3.76 (above), powered a five-car local at Bouklovtzi in May, 1965. The initial digits on these engines were their numbers; the 76 indicated 76 cm. gauge.

Three photos, Nils Huxtable   Above, D. Trevor Rowe

Maffei turned out approximately eighty-seven large two-cylinder Gölsdorf compounds for the BDZ in 1909; the entire class was re-built into simple operation after 1925. A late survivor was No. 28.77 (above) at Stanki Dmitrov on June 25, 1974. The G-12 Decapod of the Prussian State Railways was constructed to a total of 1,158 engines during the 1917-1921 era. A rugged machine, with three cylinders and Belpaire firebox, No. 13.29 (below) was awaiting her next assignment at Sofia on May 4, 1964. Three *Reichshahn* austerity 2-10-0 types included the well-known *Kriegsloks;* the 265 which arrived from Germany, Austria and the Soviet Union forming the most numerous single class of steam locomotives on the BDZ. These hard-

working Decapods outlasted more sophisticated designs through the transition period from steam to electric and diesel traction, and they constituted the bulk of the stored strategic steam reserves, held for emergency in yards throughout the country. No. 15.247 (upper left) was one of the engines acquired from the USSR, shown at Kaspican in 1965. The German class 42 heavy 2-10-0, represented by BDZ No. 16.05 (lower left) near Turnovo in 1965, saw limited use in Bulgaria, with thirty-three on the roster. They were among the last steamers to be retired in a land whose locomotives had succeeded in overcoming the most difficult challenges of terrain and economics.

Three photos, D. Trevor Rowe   Above, Nils Huxtable

RUMANIA

Rumania's railways are a reflection of her own chequered history. For eighty years, the country waxed and waned according to the fortunes of war. As a result, the *Calle Ferrate Romane* (CFR) was bequeathed a wide variety of locomotives by Austria, Hungary and Russia, and until Rumania's borders were stabilized following the Second World War, the State Railway relied heavily on locomotive manufacturers in Germany and Austria to satisfy its motive-power needs. This explains in part why so few locomotives were designed expressly for the CFR. In fact, most of the engines turned out by Rumanian builders were patterned after types in existence elsewhere.

Aside from one railway acquired from the Ottoman Empire in 1878, the first line in Rumania proper, from Bucharest to Giurgiu on the Danube, opened in 1869. Part of the direct route to Istanbul, this and other railroads came under government control twenty years later. The CFR flourished, having already established connections with Russia, Hungary and Austria, which were important to its progress and prosperity. From those countries, the Treaty of Trianon in 1918 confiscated entire provinces and gave them to Rumania. It was the break-up of the Austro-Hungarian Empire and its railways which proved to be the greater boon, since the trackage and rolling stock ceded by Russia had to be re-gauged, a task taking years to complete.

The CFR adopted great numbers of locomotives, mostly of Hungarian origin, including 2-6-2Ts, 2-8-2Ts, 2-6-2s, 4-6-2s and even 2-6-6-0 compound Mallets. While these were added to the roster in abundance, they were not regarded by the CFR as being standard types. The railway had decided earlier which designs it would utilize, and they were, for the most part, modelled on existing Prussian and Austrian engines. The famous P8 4-6-0 was a favorite, as were the freight versions, the G8 0-8-0 and G10 0-10-0. Austrian 0-10-0s were also copied, along with a set of magnificent "skyliner" 2-8-4s, the largest express power in CFR service. Purely Rumanian types (many of which were built abroad) were few, the most noteworthy being the graceful four-cylinder compound Pacifics from Henschel and Maffei, based on the Bavarian 4-6-2. They could be found on express trains over the route of Rumania's first railway as late as 1973. Škoda supplied some Moguls and Consolidations, while Rumania's own Reşiţa factory brought out a series of 2-6-2Ts. Also home-built were a pair of 2-10-2s, a freight variant of the 2-8-4.

During the early 1940s, Rumania lost her World War I territorial acquisitions, regaining only Transylvania in 1947. In the post-war era, the only new steam locomotives to come to the constricted network were two *Reichsbahn* standard 2-10-0 types: the 150.10 52 class *Kriegslok* and the 150 (DR class 50). Reşiţa continued to turn out its own handsome version of the Decapod until the late 1950s, when all steam production ceased. Shortly thereafter, the CFR began an intensive modernization program; a little over a decade later, the Pacifics and Berkshires were retired by diesel and electric traction. By 1980, hundreds of Rumanian engines were rusting in dead lines, but a few old 4-6-0s and 0-10-0s, plus the post-war 2-10-0s, could be found switching yards, handling a

few ballast and freight turns or taking out an occasional passenger train. The stars of CFR steam-power had fallen, and the rest followed within a few short years.

In Rumania, as in other East European countries, railroad photography was frowned upon, although some – but not all – enthusiasts found the situation improved by the 1970s. Just when one thought one knew what to expect, there could arise the unexpected, such as the amusing encounter which befell co-author Ziel in Timișoara, an important rail center and, less than twenty years later, the setting for the popular rebellion which spread to overthrow the Communist regime. Observing a pair of 2-6-2s puttering about the yard, he entered the office of the station master and asked the hopeful question: "photografier lokomoteev?" Staring at the questioner's 4- by 5-inch camera, the official responded clearly in three languages: "Nein, nyet, no!" Noticing several poor magazine reproductions of steam locomotives under the glass covering the desk, the author produced some of his own color postcards of steam trains. The man studied them for five minutes before realizing that they were a gift. Moments later, the assistant station master was escorting Ziel on a two-hour photographic tour of the yard, and when he returned to thank the boss, his postcards had been placed beneath the desk-top glass.

While the watchman at a rural crossing near Sagu stood at his post, a Rumanian-built P8, No. 230.256 (below), worked a heavy ore train along the well-ballasted line on October 19, 1974.

Ron Ziel

The Prussian G 10 0-10-0s, both those of DR origin and those newly-built for the CFR, became the most numerous of all steam locomotives in Rumania, with a total of 790 in service. Equally competent as medium-tonnage freight engines or as heavy shunters, they seemed to be everywhere, right up to the end of standard-gauge steam operations. In the yard at Piteşti, the crew of a G 10 began shouting at the photographer, who naturally feared immediate arrest. Once the engine came to a halt, every railroad man within sight came running over – to pose in front of No. 50.200 (below) and offer a cab ride! Four years later, in 1974,

No. 50.506 (above) was switching an army base near Dej, when the author noted both crewmen on the left side of the cab. By leaving his car on the right side, he was able to get this photo unnoticed by the railwaymen or the guards at the entrance to the base, whose view of his transgression was blocked by the engine. The yard at Oradea was teeming with steam activity on October 20, 1974, when Nos. 50.110 and 50.390 (opposite), coupled back-to-back, were weaving through the crossovers as a sister G 10 worked past the station.

Three photos, Ron Ziel

While certain German locomotive types – particularly the 2-10-0s – were to wander over much of Eastern Europe, the popular Prussian 4-6-0 went in large numbers only to Poland and Rumania, where they became the principal power for secondary passenger trains. Actually, the CFR purchased just fifty of the P 8s from Prussia; the remaining 326 on the roster were built especially for CFR service, mostly by Rumanian factories Malaxa and Reşiţa. Designated class 230 (Axle arrangement determines the European classification of steam locomotive types.), they were found in abundance in many parts of the country, even in 1974, months after the last of the larger, faster and more sophisticated 4-6-2 and 2-8-4 express classes had been withdrawn. Reflecting the brilliant orange glow of a setting October sun, No. 230.014 (upper right) was about to depart from Sagu. With gleaming brass bands around her stack and boiler jacket, No. 230.509 (above) was at Zalau, and No. 230.048 (left) was pulling a branch line local at Mirşid. On July 15, 1980, No. 230.322 (lower right) worked through a scenic valley at Drăgeşti in Crisana Province, between Transylvania and the Hungarian border.

Three photos, Ron Ziel   Lower right, Nils Huxtable

The best-known of CFR steam locomotives was the 142-class Berkshire, adapted from the Austrian 214 Class, of which thirteen had been built. By the time that the Rumanian builders were done, they had turned out seventy-nine of the 2-8-4s between 1937 and 1940. Big and powerful, they were assigned to the fastest, heaviest express trains until the coming of the diesels and electrification, nearly thirty years later. Speeding out of Bucharest in 1961, No. 142.075 (below) towered over its ten-car train at Dirza. The trimmed hedges and flower urns got a good steaming as No. 142.039 (left) pulled out of the main station at Sibiu in 1970. With most of her sisters already retired, No. 142.058 (opposite) was still an aristocrat of the rails in her shining black livery, with red running-gear and white tires, as she stood ready to leave Oradea with a stopping train to Cluj in June 1972.

Above, Ron Ziel

Below, A. E. Durrant   Opposite, Nils Huxtable

Although the Rumanian State Railways had its own classification system for steam locomotives ordered from both domestic and foreign builders, it kept the original class and road numbers on locomotives acquired second-hand, such as former MÁV 2-6-2T No. 375.929 (below), the yard switcher at Lotru, in November 1970. In 1900, the first of 2,055 Prussian T 9.3s was built; the compact 2-6-0T with medium-size driving wheels, was well-suited to light freight duties. One of these engines, CFR No. 7330 (upper right), was still active at Pascavi on June 21, 1972. Rumanian-designed and built by Reşiţa during the first three years of World War II, the big 131 class 2-6-2Ts were originally intended to replace the much smaller Hungarian 375s, but there was ample work to keep both types active until late in the final steam years. The prototype of the sixty-five built, No. 131.001 (lower right) arrived at Arad on September 16, 1963, the ornate script on Reşiţa's builder plate clearly visible on the steam dome. Like the Bulgarians, CFR favored the dual firing of coal and oil in most of its steam locomotives. Tank engines so-equipped carried their coal in the usual place – the bunker behind the cab; oil being stored in the small tanks above the water cisterns alongside the boiler, as this picture clearly shows.

Occasionally, railway photographers ran afoul of the military, as happened to one of the authors at a small rural depot. The Hertz car rental agent in Bucharest had warned him to stay away from stations and other manned facilities while photographing trains. A shiny engine, reflecting the light of the setting sun, stood simmering at the head-end of a freight near the station, which was closed and boarded up, so he drove past and parked beyond an open fence. After getting the picture, he looked at his car to see several soldiers, armed with sub-machine guns, surrounding it and a horse-drawn oil tank wagon blocking the entrance. Unable to read the warning signs, he had driven right into an Army oil depot! First a Lieutenant, then a Major, were summoned, but no communication was possible until a German-speaking Colonel arrived. After seeing the suspect's locomotive pictures and being assured by the guards that just one photo of the train had been taken, the officers shook hands with the author and let him go. Other photographers were not so fortunate; a Briton spent two weeks taking pictures in 1968 while unknowingly being shadowed by the secret police. All of his film was confiscated on the last day.

Below, Ron Ziel

Opposite, top, Nils Huxtable , bottom, A. E. Durrant

About 600 MÁV 2-6-2s were sent to Rumania, where some could still be found at work in the 1970s. Retaining its original number, 324.567 (lower left) shunted at the decrepit Timişoara passenger station; the photographer being scrutinized by curious onlookers waiting on the platform in November 1970. Its Brotan boiler straddled by a water purifier, No. 324.586 (upper left) had changed little over several decades as it neared the end of its career at Arad in 1974. Prussian G8 0-8-0s, employed by the CFR in far lesser numbers, were used primarily as switchers. The crew of well-maintained No. 40.084 (above) smiled for the camera as they peddled through the yard at Sibiu in October 1974. Among the last of the 100 2-8-0s built for the CFR by Škoda in the early 1920s, No. 140.256 (below) shunted at Vadu Crisului, also in the autumn of 1974.

Four photos, Ron Ziel

Above, J. B. Snell

Below, Ron Ziel

Above, A. E. Durrant

Below, Ron Ziel

Malaxa built two large, impressive 2-10-2 freight engines with streamlined skyline casing in 1939, but World War II prevented any more being ordered. In July 1968, No. 151.002 (opposite, top) wheeled a wreck train south of Cluj. The line across the Carpathian Mountains in Transylvania, between Hateg and Caransebes, was so steep that it required a rack section worked by seven ample 2-8-2Ts with four cylinders; the pair on the outside driving the adhesion wheels, while those inside the frame operated the rack pinions. Built by Floridsdorf in 1908, several of the powerful – but slow – engines survived into the 1970s. One engineer strenuously objected to any photographs being taken of his glistening charge, despite pleas and appeals to reason. Once the fireman had finished wiping down the locomotive and polishing the brass work, the engineer smiled and said: "Ja, ja, photo, good!" The engine, No. 40.005 (opposite, bottom), the rack gear clearly visible between the widely-spaced first and second driving wheels, was at Bucova, heading towards the rack section on October 24, 1974. 1884-vintage Hungarian 0-6-0 No. 326.062 (above) shunted at Blaj in 1961, its 77th year. Venerable Austrian 0-10-0 No. 50.012 (below), unusual in that the fourth – rather than the third – set of driving wheels mounted the main rods, chugged defiantly past a broken-down diesel at Oraviţa in 1980.

Above, A. E. Durrant

Opposite: above, C. Gammell; below, Ron Ziel

Between 1918 and 1920, CFR acquired eighty Austrian 0-10-0s, plus a few more from Poland in 1939. Useful as these locomotives were, the Prussian G10 soon became the preferred engine, being heavier, with taller wheels (for higher speeds) and a boiler that could be interchanged with the growing numbers of P8 Ten-wheelers. It seemed odd, yet fortunate, that by 1980, when the G10s were being retired by the hundreds, a few of the sixty-year-old Austrian engines still worked the tight curves and steep grades of the line between Oraviţa and Anina, in the extreme southwestern region of Rumania, probably because the larger German engines could not meet the weight and curvature restrictions. Grimy and rusty, No. 50.072 (opposite, bottom) could still put on quite a show as she blasted out of a tunnel in the Carpathian Mountains at Gradişte, with a passenger train on July 17, 1980. While the 142 class 2-8-4s were the best-known CFR power, the unusual Maffei Pacifics, also retired by the mid-1970s, were of even greater interest. Ninety were built in Germany (sixty by Maffei, thirty by Henschel) for the CFR between

1913 and 1922, and their service lives, spent pulling fast inter-city expresses and locals, were long; most of the 4-6-2s were over a half-century old when sidelined. Their appearance, while formidable and racy, was odd in that in order to shorten their wheelbase, the cylinders had to be mounted above the lead axle, rather than in the usual position; between the axles of the front bogie. This resulted in the driving rods being coupled to the first set of driving wheels, rather than the second, as is normal with most 4-6-2 designs. Seen at Dirza, speeding a light five-car express out of Bucharest on May 15, 1961, No. 231.065 (above) exhibited her cone-shaped smokebox door, polished valve covers and the four cylinders. The trailing axle was also in an unorthodox position, behind the firebox, rather than under it, thus making room for a wider firebox between the last coupled axle and the trailing axle. On October 9, 1967, a pair of Pacifics (opposite, top) double-headed a fast express from Bucharest North, the gold bands around their stacks glistening in the Autumn sunshine.

182

The World War II German 52 class *Kriegslokomotiven* wound up in every East-bloc country, including Rumania, which, as an ally of the Third Reich early in the conflict, received one hundred during the war; an additional twenty-three being left behind by the retreating *Wehrmacht* in 1944. Photographer Durrant best describes the circumstances under which he took the fine action photo (right): "Eastbound over the Carpathian Mountain range, I stopped and waited while 2-8-4 No. 142.013 backed onto the *Bucharest Express* at Turnu Severin. Then Decapod No. 150.1045 backed onto the front and *another*, No. 150.1119 (both DR 52s), took the lead to create the triple-header seen departing in September 1963." Mountain railroading in Rumania could be a spectacular proposition during the Age of Steam! Rivalling the Czech 556 class 2-10-0 in well-proportioned robustness, CFR's final steam endeavor, its version of the DR 50 class 2-10-0, complete with large smoke-deflectors and streamlined snowplow-style cowcatcher, was an aristocrat of a freight engine. The CFR rostered about 282, most of them home-built, with some having come from the DR. No. 150.106 (below) was trundling out of a receding downpour at Bābeni, its steam exhaust highlighted by the dark clouds on October 22, 1974. At Vadu Crisului, the driver of No. 150.181 (lower right) looked back expectantly as he awaited a clear signal. The Reşiţa builder's plate, prominently displayed on the smoke deflector, was dated 1957, signifying that this locomotive was one of the final batch to be erected by the famed works. The cabs of most CFR locomotives mounted no fewer than five separate cast-iron plates on each side, indicating: maximum allowable speed (km. per hour), details concerning most recent heavy repairs and depot allocation (No. 150.181s plate reads "Ord", for Oradea.), with larger CFR and number plates above. The coal and oil dual firing system, perfected by Rumanian engineer H. Cosmovici, enabled the CFR (and BDZ) to take advantage of the most desirable benefits of both fuels. The basic fire was a typical bed of hot coals, fed by hand-firing. When more power – therefore, greater steam capacity – was required, a steam jet was used to spray oil into the firebox, igniting immediately, allowing the locomotive to sustain higher speeds, assault steep grades or pull a heavier train. The position of the oil tank was usually above the water tank, right behind the coal bunker, as many of the photos in this chapter clearly show.

Above, A. E. Durrant

Two lower photos, Ron Ziel

185

In the early morning of July 14, 1980, No. 150.026 (upper left) shunted the yard at Salişte. In addition to the CFR narrow-gauge lines, which were mostly 76 cm. (approximately 30 inches), there were many forestry railways, the main function of which was to bring logs into the mills or to transfer timber to standard-gauge cars. One of the interesting lines was based at Voislova, where 0-8-0T No. 764.222, built by M. K. Államvasutak of Hungary in 1910, and No. 763.217 (below), an 0-6-0T from the same builder in 1907, worked the muddy yard in 1974. Much more modern, 0-8-0T No. 764.005 (above) came from Reşiţa in 1950. No. 764.222 (lower left), with battered buckets hanging in front, clattered over the standard-gauge crossing, on its way to the forestlands outside of Voislova.

Upper left, Nils Huxtable

Three photos, Ron Ziel

The principal narrow-gauge CFR branches were originally operated by the MÁV. The old Austrian and Hungarian engines on those lines were gradually retired in deference to uniform 0-8-0s and 0-8-0Ts from Reşiţa, as well as Polish and German builders. By the 1970s, most of these comparatively modern machines had been relegated to stand-by status by diesels on some lines, with closures rendering many other steamers surplus. Still other lines were being standard-gauged, but some of the newer engines worked into the early 1980s. Modern outside plate-frame 0-8-0 No. 764.202 (upper left) ran on the branch out of Alba Iulia, here crossing what is perhaps the lightest – as well as the cheapest – railroad bridge ever constructed, comprising just two rails supporting the track! Photographed at Sard six years later, in July 1980, sister No. 764.204 (lower left) worked the line during its last days, with the replacement standard-gauge track already in position, awaiting final alignment and grading. A German *lok* of 1923, No. 764.004 (above), on the Tirgu Mures system, where it is shown taking water in 1966. A 1900-era 0-6-0 was No. 389.001 (below), still retaining its MÁV number as it powered a passenger train at Sibiu Agnita, also in 1966. CFR narrow-gauge numbering was simple: the 764 meant 76 cm., four axles under the engine; 763 indicated three axles (0-6-0) and so forth.

Opposite, Ron Ziel   Above and below, D. Trevor Rowe

Many of the CFR forestry locomotives were fitted with balloon stacks housing spark arresters; steam-power in the timberlands was an acute fire hazard. No. 764.458 (above), an 0-8-0T, was ambling through the woods outside Stilpeni on a weed-grown right-of-way in 1980. A sister engine (left) was being fired up in the dark, sooty shed at the Stilpeni terminal. Small, ancient and tall-stacked, No. 395.005 (upper right) paused for a drink on the Alba Iulia-Zlatna branch line on September 14, 1966. To commemorate a century of steam railroads in Rumania, a large outdoor museum, exhibiting a great variety of both standard and narrow-gauge steam locomotives, was established at Reşiţa. Set in a dowdy park (lower right), the collection of engines had a common ancestry, all having been built by the factory in the background. By the late 1980s, steam on the *Calle Ferrate Romane* was virtually finished, the trains of the newly-freed nation riding behind electric and diesel locomotives.

Three photos, Ron Ziel   Upper right, D. Trevor Rowe

NORTH KOREA

Opposite: top, Sylvia Estandarte-Breva; bottom, Florian Schmidt

The railway age came to Korea in 1899 (four years after the beginning of half a century of Japanese occupation) with the construction of the Seoul-Inchon line, followed by Seoul-Pusan in 1904. After defeating the Russians in the 1904-05 war, the Japanese rushed a 500 km. railway north from Seoul to Pyongyang and the Chinese border, completing the line in just thirteen months! After 1910, many branch lines were constructed. When Japan was defeated in World War II, Korea was divided at the 38th parallel, between the Republic of Korea (ROK) in the South and the Democratic People's Republic of Korea (DPRK) in the North; the latter a Communist dictatorship under Soviet – and by 1950, Red Chinese – influence. When the DPRK government was established under Soviet occupation in 1948, its railroads consisted of 3,900 km. of track, 500 steam locomotives, 1,280 passenger and 9,154 freight cars.

Modernization was halted, then accelerated, by the Korean War of 1950-53, when Allied air attacks and fierce ground fighting destroyed most of the rail system and its rolling stock. Both the USSR and the PRC helped rebuild the *Zoson Cul Minzuzui Inmingonghoagug* (ZC) – North Korean Railways – during and after the fighting, and Chinese-built mo-

Above and below, Ian D. Johnson

tive power predominated in the postwar era. In the 1970s, the government of Kim Il-Sung, further isolating itself from the rest of the world, adopted a policy of self-reliance. This included the construction of huge hydroelectric projects to provide for the rapid electrification of the railroad system. Over 1,500 km. of new rail routes reinforced the ZC's important role in the DPRK economy.

The earliest steam locomotives on the Korean peninsula came from the U.S., followed by Japanese colonial designs, and after the Korean War, Chinese and second-hand Russian examples. Some of the older classes are known to have been in service in the early 1990s. During the conflict of the 1950s and the ensuing reconstruction, twenty-five Czech 4-8-2s, twenty Hungarian 4-8-0s and three Polish 2-6-2s were sent to Korea; some were still working recently. Despite electrification, it was estimated that as late as 1993, 400 steam locomotives were at work, mostly on branch line and shunting duties, as well as in industrial service. However, because of the modern image the late Kim Il-Sung was trying to promote, steam power was specifically banned from the capital city of Pyongyang and the surrounding area. While groups of railway photographers from England and Continental Europe have been allowed to visit, U.S. citizens are forbidden to travel to the DPRK, by both the U.S. and North Korean authorities.

In a setting typical of Stalinist monument-building, Chinese-built JF 2-8-2 No. 6131 (above) stands at the entrance to a large dam at Nampo in 1992. The plaque on the cab of spotlessly-maintained No. 172 (left) reveals that the great leader, Kim Il-Sung, once rode the footplate. Apparently, steam engines occasionally managed to reach the capital without his knowledge: with large smoke deflectors, No. 6063 (opposite, top) poses at Pyongyang with a pair of electrics. At the northernmost point of the DPRK, former Soviet Ye Class 2-10-0 No. 8143 (opposite, bottom) crossed the Tumen River on January 2, 1993 with a boxcar from China. When informed that the Ye Decapods were built in the U.S., a North Korean guide indignantly insisted, "No, no, the locomotive is English!"

With electrification of the North Korean railway system approaching an impressive 85%, steam is being phased out. The standard all-purpose steam class on the ZC is the Chinese JF 2-8-2 (see pages 211 and 214). One unique example is No. 6344 (above) at Wonsan; although fitted with the large smoke deflectors of a road engine, it has pilot footboards as well. The slogan above the headlight honors a "hero railwayman" – possibly the engine's regular driver. At Kaesong, a short distance from the South Korean border, two other JFs are No. 6318 (upper right) being coaled and No. 6415 (lower right) with Polish-style smoke deflectors. The coal bunkers of the tenders are covered; if left exposed, the powdery pulverized coal washes away in the heavy monsoon rains. Shown at the northern border town of Sinuiju, just across the Yalu River from Dandong, China in October, 1992, No. 172 (left) was a hybrid, of Japanese or Chinese design, with American-style headlight and knuckle coupler and a Russian cowcatcher. Narrow-gauge lines wound through the hills of both Koreas. In the North, a Czech-built 0-6-0T, No. 414 (below), crossed a bridge on the 762 mm. line at Hyaengsan.

Three photos, Ian D. Johnson   Opposite, Sylvia Estandarte-Breva

VIETNAM

"The history of our railways reflects the history of our country." So say the Vietnamese, whose transportation network has been so closely associated with political developments. Beginning with the French colonial administration late in the 19th Century, what was to become the *Duong Sat Vietnam* – the Vietnam Railways – (DSVN) took decades to complete. Impeding development were the First World War, the Depression and Vietnam's and the rest of Indo-China's low-priority status in the eyes of the French government. The terrain between Hanoi and Saigon (now Ho Chi Minh City) was very rugged, adding to the expense – and difficulties – of constructing the line. Finally completed in 1936, the *Ligne Imperiale Transindochinoise* (the Imperial Trans-Indo-Chinese Line) – knew just five years of peace, followed by over a third-century of almost constant warfare.

World War II, the Japanese occupation and Allied attacks inflicted much damage, followed immediately by the fighting in which the Communist Viet Minh finally ousted the French in 1954, resulting in partition between North and South. Guerilla warfare over the next decade put large sections of railway in the South out of action, and with the entry of the United States into the morass, aerial attacks severely crippled the rail system in the North. It was only on

Above, Günter Oczko   Below, Werner Reber   Upper right, Neil J. Edwards

the railroads of Vietnam and North Korea that steam beneath the red star suffered combat losses during the forty-five years of the Cold War.

The end of the Vietnam War in the mid-1970s resulted in the slow re-building of the entire rail system, which consists of two distinct parts: a network of branchlines radiating from the capital of Hanoi and the 1,726 km Hanoi-Ho Chi Minh City *Thong Nhat* ("Reunification Line"), running the length of the country. The Communist administration of the People's Republic of Vietnam has been extensively re-building and modernizing, with the result that steam traction may be phased out in the 1990s. Initially, most locomotives were produced in France, with some Swiss and German examples arriving in the 1920s. Japanese engines dating from World War II were still running in the last years of steam, and China supplied 2-8-2s during the Vietnam War, to aid the North in its efforts to conquer the South.

Except for the famed Dalat Rack Line, few steam locomotives were to survive the Vietnam War in the South, and it was only afterwards that a few locomotives were sent down from Hanoi. By the late 1980s, Western railway photographers were being welcomed – just in time to obtain some memorable images of steam in action on the *Duong Sat Viet Nam*.

It would seem that a developing nation comes of age industrially when it manages to erect a couple of steam locomotives in its own shops, as Turkey did, prior to dieselizing. Vietnam accomplished the same thing, building a pair of 2-8-2s, later using one to power a train north from Saigon and the other south from Hanoi, to participate in ceremonies re-opening the cross-country route. Home-built No. 141-122 (opposite) pulled a freight at Giap Bat, in 1989. At Hai Duong, where old wooden crossties as well as concrete ones supported the rails, No. 131-444 (above) hauled a two-car train. No. 141-179 (below) gave a farmer and his water buffalo a steam bath on the Nam Dinh line on September 30, 1987.

While the DSVN is meter-gauge, the line from Gia Lam to the Chinese border was widened to dual-gauge during 1963-1968, to expedite the movement of war materiel from the Communist bloc. The Chinese supplied an unknown number of their *Jiefang 6* 2-8-2s to the Vietnamese, who called them *Giai Phong 6* (both terms meaning "Liberation"). GP-6 1055 (above) at Luu Xa on November 12, 1989 and GP-6 1013 (below) in Hanoi were among the last survivors of the 1930s and '40s era

engines. The 131-class 2-6-2Ts were of the Japanese C-12-type, brought to Indo-China during World War II. One of the few remaining in service at the end of steam took water at Hai Duong, while a 1960s Chinese-built Mikado, No. 141-189 (upper right) waited its turn at the plug. Among the last of the French 2-8-2s, No. 141-108 (lower right) powered a passenger train alongside a road and a canal at Phu Ly in March, 1991.

Three photos, Neil J. Edwards   Lower right, Florian Schmidt

Above, Günter Oczko

Between twenty-five and thirty 2-8-2s designed by the great French engineer André Chapelon arrived in Vietnam between 1948 and 1952, many of which wound up in the North after the Communist victory. No. 141-108 (above), the gold star and red circle emblem of the Peoples Republic on the smoke deflector, led a Hue-Hanoi freight near Tia on March 19, 1989, having survived two wars. Returning to its train in the dual-gauge yard at the Chinese border after servicing, No. GP-6 1019 (below) was rusty and grimy, like most DSVN engines, on February 26, 1993. Japanese-built 2-6-2T No. 131-428 (right) at the Haiphong depot on March 22, 1990 was the last of her class to see service.

Below, M. Clendining

Right, Florian Schmidt

201

The most remarkable steam locomotives ever built for the railways of Indo-China were undoubtedly the Chapelon Pacifics. Designed for passenger service, the first series of ten engines (class 231-300) was delivered by SACM-Graffenstaden in 1933. Forty-five locomotives of a heavier and more powerful version (class 231-500) – by the same builder and Haine-St. Pierre – were supposed to follow between 1939 and 1948, but half a dozen were diverted elsewhere. Phased out of service in 1988, two of the last active 4-6-2s, Nos. 231-531 (left, above) and 231-530 (left, below) – with No. 141-186 in the background, were running out their last kilometers in Hanoi the previous year. These Belpaire firebox Pacifics possesed a very Gallic-American appearance, as did the meter-gauge Mikados, with their French-style smokebox door mounts and U.S.-type headlights, couplers and cowcatchers. A locomotive incident of the mid-1980s involving the DSVN highlighted the weird, wasteful and incredible incompetence of bureaucracy which ignores the realities of the world. To show solidarity with their "fraternal comrades" in Southeast Asia, the Soviet Railways rounded up ten retired TE-class (DR 52) 2-10-0s from their standard-gauge lines around Kaliningrad and sent them to Vietnam (probably by an 11,000-miles sea journey). The Polish State Railways did the same with three identical Ty-2s. Once in Vietnam, it was discovered that the Decapods were too heavy for the light track and that they were in other ways unsuitable for operation on the DSVN. Years later, they were dumped at three different yards, never even having been fired up! Meanwhile, as time was running out for Vietnamese steam-power, the main shops at Hanoi continued to perform major overhauls on the diminishing stock. On March 25, 1990, a Chinese-built 2-8-2 with somewhat rakish triangular-shaped smoke deflectors, No. 141-152 (above), received heavy repairs. Less than six months previously in the same building, French-built No. 141-103 and Chinese Nos. 141-209 and 210 (right) were undergoing light running repairs. Its relations with the West improving by the mid-1990s, the Vietnamese were seeking to end the last vestiges of their long period of conflict by forging closer ties with the United States as well. Greater access to international markets and funding would mean a quick end to steam operations on the DSVN, since the urge to "modernize" always seems to seize the political high ground with emerging countries, even if such policies do not always follow logical economic practice. By 1994, only fifty steam locomotives on both meter and standard gauges remained in service, while more than twice as many diesels were operating.

Above, Florian Schmidt

Opposite, Werner Reber   Right, Neil J. Edwards

CHINA

In the late-1970s, with the phasing out of steam traction in the other "Red Star" countries, the opening of the People's Republic of China to Westerners came just in time. The visiting enthusiasts found a heavily-trafficked railroad system more than 80% dependent on steam. Pacifics were assigned to many expresses, and a ceaseless parade of big 2-10-2s monopolized freights on double-track mainlines. With 2-8-2s and 2-10-2s still being mass-produced, China was hailed as "the land of 10,000 steam locomotives."

At the time of Mao Tse-tung's 1949 so-called "Liberation" of China, the Ministry of Railways controlled a much-ravaged network originally financed by foreign interests, including the United States, Britain, Russia and other European powers. During their 1930s occupation of Manchuria, when they re-gauged the Russian lines, the Japanese invested heavily, as did the Chinese themselves. Expansion and modernization had been retarded by decades of warfare, as well as the revolution; barely half of the 12,000 route-miles remained serviceable in 1949. Enforced political stability stiffened the resolve of the new regime to forge a comprehensive network serving all of China. Among the achievements of Chinese railway builders during the immediate post-revolutionary period were the lines from Chongching to Chengdu and Chengdu to Baoji.

The disparate origins of China's railroads were reflected in its pre-1950 locomotive stock, supplied by the countries which had financed the system. Of course, the Cold War only served to intensify the determination of China to become self-sufficient in locomotive production. Initially, existing designs such as the JF 1 2-8-2 and the SL 6 4-6-2 were simply duplicated in China's own workshops. Within a decade after the Communist victory, locomotive construction in China was well into its stride, with Russian-influenced standard designs rolling out of the plants at Qingdao, Datong and Dalian. While making for more efficient operation and maintenance, standardization brought about the retirement of many interesting engines, including such exotic classes as the streamlined Japanese-built SL 7 Pacifics of *Asia Express* fame.

But standardization could not save steam – even in China. Despite cheap labor, abundant coal reserves and the low cost of home-built 2-10-2s (one-third that of comparable diesels), new mainline steam construction ceased at Datong in 1988. While limited production of light SY 2-8-2s for industrial use was to continue into the 1990s, the future had been decided in favor of dieselization and electrification; a decision based partially on the socialist view of "modernization", which had no place for steam-power, economically viable

though it still was. The pace of steam retirement was so rapid that nearly-new engines were being withdrawn, and officials were proudly predicting the elimination of mainline steam by the turn of the century.

By the early 1990s, tour operators were already promoting "Farewell to Steam in China" packages. Unlike the former Soviet Union, China had come to regard railway interest with bemused tolerance; indeed, steam operations had become a tourist attraction in the Northeast (Manchuria), where government travel brochures included color photos of an Anglo-American group of "steam locomotive lovers" photographing 2-10-2s. Apart from a few isolated incidents involving arrests in "restricted" areas, the independent traveler was able to visit a growing number of remote lines. With a smattering of Mandarin, a taste for Chinese cuisine and a disregard for creature comforts, the adventurous enthusiast could buy a train ticket, leave the dieselized mainlines far behind, arrive in a junction town and spend days photographing a procession of double-headed freights. The reaction of engine crews to the appearance of a foreign photographer at the lineside was usually a friendly wave and a smile – a marked contrast to the "manacled wrists" gesture favored in Yugoslavia! The steam seekers who visited China in the 1980s felt fortunate to have experienced the pageant of American-style big-steam operations on a scale never to be seen again, anywhere in the world.

Opposite, Pete Skelton   Right, Nils Huxtable

Sub-zero temperatures in northern China attracted the most hardy photographers, often rewarding them with spectacular results, such as QJ 2-10-2s Nos. 6743 and 2497 (opposite) on the Zhongwei-Gantang line on January 21, 1992. In milder form, the artistry of winter decorated a JF 2-8-2 (right) at Changchun in 1989.

Once standard designs for 2-8-2 medium and 2-10-2 heavy freight power had been developed, the Chinese locomotive designers refined the SL 4-6-2. The appropriately-named *Ren Min* (People's) Pacific was compact yet powerful, augmenting older types and facilitating the rapid expansion of the rail system. An integral part of the passenger fleet for over a quarter of a century, all were retired by the early 1990s. In what is believed to have been the first multiple flash night photo of a Chinese locomotive, RM No. 1182 (above) was ready to depart the main station in Taiyuan on December 1, 1981. The heavy train, consisting of thirteen cars, was no problem for the brawny Pacific. Already in place above the 4-6-2 are the carrying cables for the ongoing electrification which would soon make No. 1182 and many of her sisters redundant. The

crew of RM No. 1168 (upper right), coupled behind QJ 2-10-2 No. 581, bantered with twenty photographers on the platform at Baimashan, a suburban station of Jinan, several days later. For sheer quantity of steam operations, few places matched Changchun, a busy junction on the Beijing-Harbin line, boasting a locomotive works, roundhouse, a huge yard and more than a hundred daily steam arrivals and departures. Her blow-down valve discharging a fifty-foot-long cloud of steam as she entered the yard at sunset, RM No. 1183 (lower right) was heading the twenty-second of twenty-six steam-powered trains to pass the east end of Changchun Yard in five hours, on September 21, 1988. Soon diesels began to intrude, drastically curtailing steam operations.

Three photos, Ron Ziel

With the temperature far below freezing, RM No. 1142 (upper left), a red star on her smokebox, sped through Xiaonan in January, 1989. In the late 1950s, as thousands of steam locomotives became surplus in the Soviet Union, China alleviated its motive-power shortage by purchasing more than 1,000 FD 2-10-2s from the Russians. Initially called the *You Hao* or "Friendship" class, they were re-gauged; later they regained their FD classification. Once China was turning out its own QJ 2-10-2 in large numbers, the FDs were retired; all had gone by the mid-1980s. Their last areas of operations were around Wuhan, Shanghai and Guilin. FD No. 1600 (below) wheeled a coal drag through Suzhou on December 10, 1981. Several days later, FD 1348 (right), with metal cut-out red flag on her smoke deflector, and FD 1067 (lower left) worked the line at the Shanghai suburb of Xui Jia Hui.

Opposite: top, Nils Huxtable; bottom, Thomas R. Schultz
Above and below, Ron Ziel

The world's last standard-gauge regular-service steam locomotive still in production during the 1990s was the modest but versatile SY class 2-8-2, used mostly for heavy industrial work around mines and large factories. SY No. 0001 (above), the prototype of more than 1,800 erected by 1994, was under steam at the Taiyuan shed in 1981. Sisters Nos. 0071 and 0984 (opposite, top) worked at Mengjiatun in February of 1989. An interesting postscript to the story of the otherwise humble and unremarkable SY: in the late 1980s, three of them (plus the last-built larger JS 2-8-2) were constructed especially for operation on preservation lines in the United States. The managements of the American shortlines concerned had found that even at a price of more than $300,000 each (plus shipping), these engines were bargains com-

pared to the expense of re-building existing U.S. locomotives which had not run in thirty years. Only two of the SYs made it to their destinations; the third one wound up on the seabed of the Indian Ocean when the ship carrying it sank in a storm. On New Years Day, 1993, well-decorated yet grimy GJ 0-6-0T No. 1013 (opposite, bottom) trundled past an American-style coaling tower with a newly-shopped tender from a JS in tow, at Sujiatun. The downgrading of road engines to shunting service has been practiced in many countries, including China, which utilized many medium-size JF 2-8-2s in yard service. The tender of one of them, No. 2422 (below), was "kit-bashed" into a four-wheel affair for shed pilot duties at Changchun. At a cursory glance, the 2-8-2 looked like a tank engine.

Upper left and right, Mike Eagleson   Center left and below, Ron Ziel

When the Chinese needed a lighter locomotive than the 2-8-2 for industrial work, they decided on a compact 2-6-2 design, classified YJ. Confined mainly to factory yards and mineheads, the little Prairie-types seldom worked elsewhere. YJ No. 273 (top left) and No. 272 (top right) were switching the Kailuan Coal Mine yard at Tangshan on March 29, 1983. The Tangshan steam locomotive factory was destroyed by an earthquake in July, 1976, then later rebuilt. American-made United Nations Relief and Rehabilitation Administration 2-8-0s, exported to China shortly before the Communist victory over the Guomindang in 1949, were not seen again by Westerners until the re-opening of China nearly thirty years later. They were the last Consolidations in mainline service in China. KD7 No. 505 (lower right) worked a passenger train at Shanghai in 1981, and No. 575 (above) was coupled to a local freight at Hangzhou, on October 4, 1988.

212

Reflecting their triumph, the Communists named their earlier 2-8-2 class the *Jia Fang* ("Liberation") and 4-6-2 type *Sheng Li* ("Victory"); a fair number of both engines surviving into the 1980s. Most of the Mikados had been demoted to yard switching, including JF Nos. 2282 and 1274 (lower left), working as hump engines at Datong in November, 1981. Some still handled line work and retained their road pilots, as did No. 2381 (upper left), accelerating a short freight at Jinan the following month. The Japanese- and Chinese-built SL Pacifics were to become the most sought-after locomotives in the PRC by the mid-1980s, when the last survivors were running out their final miles in Manchuria. Just a few years earlier, in 1981, the old 4-6-2s were far more widespread. A rarity indeed was Giesl ejector-fitted SL No. 312 (above), wheeling a ten-car train on the outskirts of Nanjing at twilight. Sister No. 421 (right) was moving a train out of the main station, also in 1981. The original Japanese-built SLs had spoked driving wheels while later ones were fitted with Boxpoks. The Chinese ones had Boxpok drivers; all were eventually fitted with smoke deflectors. Though older, the SLs were to outlive the RMs by about a year.

SL "Victory" Pacifics proved their worth in the cold Manchurian winters right until the last ones were retired in the early 1990s. Chinese railroaders and locomotives (as well as Western photographers) fought minus forty-degrees temperatures in the biting Siberian winds and under the clearest azure skies. SL No. 664 (left) departed Bei Shan with a local for Meihekou in January, 1988. In 1990, the fireman of No. 623 (above), opened the blow-down valve at the front of the firebox.   No. 681 (below), worked her train along the Changchun-Jilin line near Xinglongshan in December, 1989.

Above and left, Nils Huxtable Below, Thomas R. Schultz

Chinese tank engines were employed as shed and works pilots as well as industrial switchers. Two of the largest steel manufacturers offered photographers the selection shown here. A pair of 0-6-0Ts at the Anshan Steel Works in 1987 included No. 485 (left) and XK2 No. 57 (below), the latter a former U.S. Army engine, which may have come to China from Eastern Europe. Baotou Steel rostered a variety of smaller power, including an ET7 0-8-0T, No. 5332 (opposite, bottom) of Polish origin, shown double-heading with 2-6-2 YJ No. 170 on April 12, 1988. A squat 0-6-0T with widely-spaced driving wheels was XK13 No. 130 (opposite, top), also at Baotou.

Four photos, Mike Eagleson

THE DATONG LOCOMOTIVE WORKS

Six photos, Ron Ziel

After the Chitteranjan locomotive factory in India ceased producing steam locomotives in 1972, only China continued to build them in large numbers – for the next sixteen years. While there were several complexes carrying out the work, the largest one at Datong, west of Beijing, turned out the heaviest locomotives in the greatest numbers; sometimes attaining a production rate of one per day. A visit to the vast facility which covered many acres and employed several thousand skilled craftsmen, was a priceless experience for Western steam enthusiasts – one to be remembered all their lives. With over 90% of production devoted to the big QJ (*Qian Jin* - "March Forward") 2-10-2, the rest being large JS (*Jian She* - "Construction") 2-8-2s, it was like visiting the famed Baldwin Locomotive Works of Philadelphia in the 1920s. One four-acre building, the floor of which was heaped with mounds of red sand, contained forms (above) into which molten steel was poured for casting frames, which were assembled (upper left) in an adjoining structure. There was a sprawling boiler plant and a section where large tubular forms (lower left) such as cylinder linings, steam delivery pipes and petticoat pipes were fabricated. Drop forges pounded out side rods, pedestal straps and drawbars. Then all of the many castings, forgings and appliances were delivered to the erecting shop to be assembled into completed locomotives (upper right) such as JS No. 6202, on November 28, 1981. The same engine's wheels (center right), as well as those of No. 6203 behind, were being readied so that the rest of the locomotive could be lifted into place. The welded tenders were assembled in another building (lower right), then coupled to the new engines, which were test-fired and run around the yard. Once any final adjustments were made, the locomotives were painted and turned over to the railway administration, to begin their service lives.

Final development of a line of 2-8-2 freight locomotives in China, the JS class also saw service on passenger trains. JS Nos. 5141 and 5771 (below) accelerated out of Hunjiang with a train to Baihe on January 29, 1992. This pair had large "elephant-ear" smoke deflectors, but others, such as No. 6061 (left) in the busy terminal at Xuchou in 1981, went without them. Also at Xuchou, JS No. 5478 (upper right), in the company of QJ No. 592, carried the smaller, high-mounted version in this night scene. Another pair of the Mikados, led by JS 5480 (lower right), worked a train at Dayangcha in February, 1989. By 1994, the JS and QJ locomotives accounted for virtually all road work and perhaps 90% of steam-powered movements in the PRC. Being the newest and most numerous of steam classes in mainline service, they may well be the only ones to remain active in the 21st Century.

Upper left, upper right, Ron Ziel
Lower left, Pete Skelton   Lower right, Nils Huxtable

The JS Mikados assigned to passenger service were generally better maintained than those engaged primarily in freight and shunting work. One example was JS No. 5431 (lower left), climbing the grade out of Nancha, on the single-track line to Wuyiling, on September 26, 1988. As JS No. 5595 worked a local freight at Xuchou, QJ 2737 (upper left) overtook her on the adjoining track. Power for the grade (above) in a photograph described by lensman Skelton as a "Triple-header spectacle west of Mengjianwan–QJs 6541, 2833, 2089, head for the horseshoe on the Zhongwei-Gantang section". Later QJs, such as the lead engine here, built after 1980, had larger capacity six-wheel-truck tenders. In mid-winter, Changchun could be a cold place indeed, as the mechanic working on a QJ (right), encrusted in frost and ice from its own condensing steam, would testify.

Opposite, Ron Ziel Above, Pete Skelton Below, Nils Huxtable

Whether at a distance or close-up, the "March Forward" 2-10-2 was an impressive and handsome freight engine. Indeed, the *Qian Jin* served as a dual-purpose machine, easily able to hold down passenger assignments if a train was too heavy for an RM or a JS. The versatile QJ accounted for nearly half of the 10,000 steam locomotives operating in the PRC in 1980, and a much higher percentage a decade later. It is believed that once the Russians suddenly terminated construction of the LV 2-10-2 in 1956, they sold the mechanical drawings and even some of the production machinery to the Chinese, who used them to build the QJ derivative. If so, the design was somewhat modified, eventually becoming one of the most prolific and successful locomotives ever built, as well as the last. Double-heading out of Datong, just a few miles from where they were built, QJ Nos. 355 and 1661 (opposite, top) sent their white exhaust into the polluted sky on a cold November 29, 1981. No. 1333 (opposite, bottom) accelerated a morning passenger train out of Taiyuan. Built in the mid-1980s, Nos. 6767 and 6541 (above), stormed around the horseshoe curve near Mengjiawan in 1992. On the long approach to the massive span across the Yangtze River at Nanjing, QJs 2517 and 3065 (right) were photographed from the highway viaduct at a point where it curves in above the railway line to form the combined bridge.

Three photos, Ron Ziel Above, Pete Skelton

There were some interesting narrow-gauge operations in China. 0-8-0s based on a 1930s Russian design were the most common power. Nos. 31 and 30 (above) are seen pulling a train of passenger cars which strongly resembled standard-gauge ones, at Langxiang on April 8, 1988. The 60 cm.-gauge line from Jiejie to Giejiu, in Yunnan Province, still ran Baldwin-built engines, including No. 19 (left) in 1989. In contrast to many European railways, which relied on small lamps, most Chinese locomotives mounted two big American-style headlights. So-fitted, QJ No. 7081 (opposite), worked through the woods near Tumenling, her own exhaust steam silhouetting the engine. The year was 1989, and the last stronghold of mainline steam in the world was already in steep decline, heralding the end of almost two centuries of steam railroading.

Above, Mike Eagleson   Below, Florian Schmidt   Opposite, Nils Huxtable

CUBA

Ron Ziel

In Cuba, the time machine appeared to have stopped in 1959 – at least in terms of American-made technology. A third of a century later, vintage automobiles – from '48 Chevrolets to '59 Chryslers – plied roads crossed and paralleled by tracks of four gauges: 27 1/2-inch, 30-inch, 36-inch and standard. In the fields of wind-rippled sugar cane and at the sprawling *centrals* (sugar mills) was another kind of American transportation museum, with operating exhibits from H. K. Porter, Rogers, Davenport, Alco, Vulcan and – above all – Baldwin. In the 1990s, with no builder's plate more recent than 1935, and some dating back more than a century, by far the largest concentration of regular-service "Made in U.S.A." steam locomotives in the world was to be found just ninety miles from Florida.

By the end of the 19th Century, sugar was becoming the world export crop of Cuba, still under Spanish rule. An extensive network of canefield railroads was being developed, but it was not until the liberation of Cuba, during the Spanish-American War of 1898, that a vast infusion of U.S. capital brought increased expansion, modernization and many locomotives to the island. The size and power of steam engines was increasing, and the new ones sent to Cuba in the early 1900s were typical of the era. World War I saw a greater demand for both Cuban sugar and the locomotives to transport the cane, but the manufacturers were already swamped with orders, so second-hand engines dating from the

1890s came from such U.S. carriers as the Southern Railway, Pittsburgh & Lake Erie, and Buffalo, Rochester & Pittsburgh. With the European sugar-beet industry severely damaged in the Great War, the sugar producers of Cuba and elsewhere aimed to satisfy the increased demand, so they expanded their capacity and built more rail lines. Baldwin was quick to respond, and if builder's plates are any indication, 1920 must have been a bumper year for 2-8-0s from Philadelphia.

In 1933, American ownership of the Cuban sugar industry – about fifty percent – was at its peak; by the time Fidel Castro came to power, many U.S.-owned sugar *centrals* had been sold to Cuban interests, including the vast holdings of the Hershey chocolate manufacturer. Many of the larger, better-financed operations were already dieselized in the 1950s. Yet, thirty-five years later, more than one-third of the nationalized *centrals* under the bureaucratic umbrella of the *Ministerio de Azúcar* (Minaz) still mustered more than 300 steam locomotives during the *zafra,* or sugar harvest, from January to May. Minaz policy was to allow each mill to determine its own motive-power requirements. Of course, keeping such antiques operating was a remarkable example of doing without and making do. If finding spare parts for a '50 Plymouth seemed a daunting prospect, what about parts for an 1894 Rogers 2-4-2T?

The sugar railroads themselves were in danger of

extinction until the early 1980s. Contributing to the decline was the traditional labor-intensive and time-consuming method of transporting cut cane to the mills – a system still employed in hilly regions. Teams of oxen hauled wagon-loads of cane to a *chucho,* a gantry equipped with pulleys for transferring the loads into the cane cars. Trucks were threatening to replace many sugar lines until the introduction of the *acopio,* a huge cane-cutting facility which, by chopping stalks into smaller pieces, separating leaves and chaff, greatly increased the efficiency of both rail or oxen and motor transport. Some *centrals* began expanding their rail lines, and one, which had abandoned its railway, went back to trains after re-laying the track.

If anything, Cuban steam owed its survival to the country's desperate economic straits. With the collapse of Communism in the Soviet Union, which, along with its satellites, had served to prop up Castro's regime by providing aid and accepting sugar in exchange for oil and other commodities, Cuba's economic problems became acute. The situation was further aggravated by the tightening of the U.S. embargo, the purpose of which was to cripple the Cuban economy, thereby toppling the regime. After the cut-off of assistance from the former Soviet bloc, everything was in short supply, and one could not help but wonder whether the rallying cry of

"Socialismo o Muerte" ("Socialism or Death") should have been *"Socialismo es Muerte"* ("Socialism is death")!

Those American enthusiasts who had gone to Cuba during the brief period that their government relaxed restrictions in the early '80s were rewarded with steam scenes long since vanished from the U.S. Railway photographers received a mixed reception. Once, when the regime was desperate for scapegoats, they were accused of spreading a disease which infects cane stalks! Policy changed, and steam aficionados (especially their dollars) were to be welcomed. Still, film confiscations could occur, mostly at the whim of a "vigilant" airport customs official. Usually, however, the photographer returned from the canefields with images of working steam in a blighted paradise. The locomotives, some past their centenary, seemed to symbolize Cuba itself, struggling to hold out against the tide of inevitable change.

With a slender blunderbuss stack taller than the boiler barrel, Davenport 0-4-0T No. 1147 (opposite) was one of the smallest standard-gauge engines and perhaps the most charming tank locomotive running anywhere. Still working the cane dumper at the Marcelo Salado Central near Remedios into the mid-1990s, she is shown here on March 28, 1981. Central Osvaldo Sanchez at Güines had both 30-inch and standard-gauge trackage. 2-6-0 No. 1507, built by Schenectady in 1912, towered over little 1920 Baldwin 2-8-0 No. 1110 (below) at the engine shed on April 5, 1980.

Nils Huxtable

While the sugar cane railroads hauled but one commodity and all of the rolling-stock looked virtually identical, the variety of locomotives and the antiquity of operations aroused a fascination rarely possible in the post-industrial age. Except for the heavy-duty rubber tires supporting the oxen-powered cane wagon, with Central Mal Tiempo line 2-8-0 No. 1238 on hand (above), this scene could just as well have been seventy years before the actual date: 1981. The sugar plantations were named after different countries, historical personages, dates of political importance and, in the case of Central Puerto Rico Libre, an obvious propaganda jab at the United States. Lounging in the cab of No. 1901 (upper left) at the latter mill, the crew await their next run. The 30-inch gauge network at the Pepito Tey Central near Cienfuegos boasted a fleet of Baldwin Moguls and Consolidations built between 1905 and 1924. 2-8-0 No. 1236 (below) was in her seventy-first year when she brought a trainload of cane fresh from the fields, past the mill and into the holding yard on February 27, 1981. Also 2 1/2-foot gauge, the Central Espartaco lines offered lush tropical scenery and a plate girder bridge over the Caunao River, right beyond one of the main cane loaders. 1915 Baldwin 2-8-0 No. 1328 (left) trundled back and forth over the bridge four times while shunting cars to make up its train, allowing ample photographic opportunities. This was one of the few narrow-gauge sugar engines equipped with modern piston-valve cylinders, a counterpoint to her crosshead water pump. The bridge piers have been meticulously bricked between the steel members, giving them a fossilized appearance. Many of the 30-inch gauge locomotives (including Nos. 1236 and 1328) were equipped with crosshead-mounted water pumps as primary water supply with the injectors only as back-up, a practice discarded by most railroads before 1900.

Upper left, Nils Huxtable   Three photos, Ron Ziel

Below, Wayne Weiss   Three photos, Ron Ziel

In 1981, when three of the locomotives on this spread were photographed, their combined ages totalled 292 years, and two of them were still performing their regular duties. Generally believed to have been the oldest locomotive still in revenue service in the Western Hemisphere, Central Rubén Martínez Villena No. 1112 (above), built by Burnham, Parry, Williams and Company (Baldwin) in 1878, was 103 years old at the time. The Cubans were well aware of the historical significance of the tiny 0-4-2T, using her to switch afew cars at a time into the cane dumper right alongside the administration building behind No. 1112. After being put on display, she was back in service in 1993! Although no longer used to push cane cars around, Central Espartaco 0-4-2T No. 1 (upper right), only the 677th locomotive to be built by H. K. Porter, was still at the mill's enginehouse at Palmira, where the 1885 veteran was spotted for photography. Central Amistad con los Pueblos still found light work for 0-4-0T No. 1106 (lower right), built by Baldwin in 1888. Clearly visible on the smokebox is a second builder's plate, indicating that the engine received a replacement boiler from Baldwin in 1928. By the time that Fidel Castro's revolution ushered in the Communist era in January 1959, some of the larger mill work shops had acquired the expertise, tools and equipment to do all of the major locomotive repair work themselves, mainly because their American suppliers had ceased manufacturing steam engine components several years previously. Later, Minaz mechanics were able to turn to the People's Republic of China for their replacement parts, and it became common to see brand-new copies of such items as Westinghouse air compressors, Monitor injectors and Pyle generators, with Chinese characters on their brass plates. One would not expect to see a tunnel in the flat sugar cane fields, but Central Esteban Hernandez's track ran through one near Martí. 2-6-2 No. 1225 (H. K. Porter, 1919) – still carrying her original No. 2 – (left) made an obstreperous exit on March 4, 1980.

As late as 1994, Marcelo Salado mill still had six *locomotoras de vapor* on the property; each one a different wheel arrangement: 0-4-0T, 0-6-0T, 2-6-2T, 2-6-0, 2-8-0, 4-6-0. A 1916 Baldwin Mogul, No. 1429 (opposite), was flying extra flags at Carolina Junction with the well-ballasted mainline of the *Ferrocarril de Cuba* (Cuban Railway), over whose trackage the larger mill engines regularly operated between the *central* and three disconnected branch lines. Also adhering to the Cuban tradition of displaying extra flags even when resting at the engine terminals, the Moguls and Consolidations of Central Amistad con los Pueblos, near Güines, had outside railings along their running boards – a standard feature on Russian and Bulgarian locomotives for over a century, but rarely seen elsewhere. 2-6-0 No. 1302 (right) loosed plumes of oil smoke into the tropical foliage and leaked steam from her cylinders, as the 1904 Alco chuffed out of the engine terminal at mid-day on March 30, 1981. No. 1303 was a twin sister built in 1905, shown with 1920 Baldwin 2-8-0 No. 1602 (below) amid the usual fascinating clutter of a short line engine shed.

Opposite, Nils Huxtable   Two photos, Ron Ziel

Two photos, Ron Ziel

Opposite, Nils Huxtable

The Vulcan Iron Works was best-known for specializing in tank engines and some small tender locomotives, but the company occasionally erected larger ones, including eighty-eight Decapods for Turkey, following World War II. Also big by Vulcan standards was 2-8-0 No. 1904 (above); the 1920-built locomotive was assigned to Central Primero de Enero, near Violeta, in 1981. Built a year later by Alco's Cooke Works, Consolidation No. 1835 (below) worked the same mill. 2-6-0 No. 1711 (opposite, top) switched a cane loader of the Central Boris Luis Santa Coloma, near Madruga, in March 1990. Baldwin built batches of Moguls for Cuba until 1925, but due to fluctuations in sugar prices, some remained in the U.S.A., including former Mobile & Gulf (now French Lick, West Baden & Southern) No. 97. Two of her identical sisters, Nos. 1530 and 1531 (opposite, bottom) gained fame in the 1980s at Central Jose Smith Comas, near Cárdenas, as perhaps the cleanest, best-maintained locomotives in all of Cuba.

Tank engines were popular on the Cuban sugar lines, particularly for switching the yards and cane dumpers at the mills. There were also some unusual specimens, such as diminutive locomotives with truncated tenders and fireless yard engines which received their steam supply from the mill boilers. A pair of typical light industrial 0-4-0T plant locos were always busy in the mill yard of Central España Republicana, near Cárdenas, during the cane-cutting season. Both built by Vulcan in 1915 and 1916 respectively, Nos. 1120 and 1121 (upper left) were shunting on February 25, 1981. The Rogers Locomotive Works of Paterson, New Jersey was renowned for the quality of its locomotives, and several of its machines survived in Cuba, including 1894-built 2-4-2T No. 1204 (left) at Central Osvaldo Sanchez, still hard at work in her ninety-sixth year, on March 5, 1990. A nondescript 0-4-0 saddle-tank was Central Eduardo García Lavandero's 1919 Baldwin No. 1104 (lower left), shown positioning a cut of loaded cars on a siding at the mill near Artemisa. Much more embellished than most humble yard tanks, large

Vulcan 0-4-2T No. 1201 (upper right) sported both an enormous headlight and a boiler-tube pilot, rather than the footboards typical of a switcher. The 1916 Vulcan worked for Central Gregario A. Mañalich, at Melena del Sur, during the 1981 *zafra* season. Another rare Rogers four-coupled engine of small dimensions and an almost Walt Disney cartoon appearance, 2-4-0 No. 1216 (right) was built in 1892 as a 2-4-4T Forney and assigned to the Central Fructuoso Rodriguez in 1990. Trailing a home-built, four-wheel, slope-back tender, and sporting a large cab, the stubby little engine carried the name "Limonar", the local political jurisdiction. "Fireless cookers" did not generate their own steam, instead receiving injections of superheated water from the huge stationary boilers which powered the mill machinery. Confined to the sidings near the boiler, a "thermos bottle" such as No. 1172 (lower right), built in Germany by Koppel in 1912, could run for hours without a recharge of steam; it was photographed at Central Ciro Redondo, near Morón.

Four photos, Ron Ziel

Center left, John B. Charles   Center right, Nils Huxtable

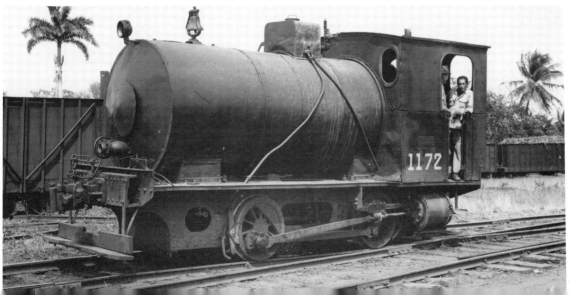

Above, John B. Charles

It is not often possible to get a full front-view photograph of a train in action, but when the cameramen are riding a gas-powered railcar directly ahead of the locomotive, it can be done. Such was the opportunity on March 28, 1981, when 36-inch gauge Baldwin 2-8-0 No. 1424 (upper left) was pulling a train of empty cane cars beneath a canopy of overhanging tree branches on its way to the fields of Central Heriberto Duquesne, near Remedios. Consolidation No. 1843 (lower left), a 1924 Baldwin, operating on the line of Central Carlos Manuel de Céspedes in March 1990, was identical to the Sierra Railroad of California's famous 2-8-0, No. 28. Another Central Osvaldo Sanchez engine was 1919-built Baldwin outside-frame 2-8-0 No. 1310 (above), shown in 1990. Henschel (1912) 2-4-0T No. 1207 (below), one of the few non-American mill locomotives in Cuba, still retained a German-style bell as she puttered about the fields of Central Rubén Martínez Villena. It is probable that 98% of the steam engines of the sugar cane lines came from United States manufacturers.

Lower left, Nils Huxtable

Upper left and below, Ron Ziel

A handsome Mogul built by Porter in 1915, whose front sandbox was increased in height at a later date, was Central Gregorio A. Mañalich No. 1108 (upper left). Although the 2-6-2 type was well-suited for sugar cane haulage, relatively few of them could be seen on Cuban rail lines. When driving on the rear coupled-axle, Prairie locomotives could be low-slung and rather ungainly, such as Central Caracas No. 1538 (above); conversely, Central Efraín Alfonso No. 1635 (lower left), was rather trim and well-proportioned. Although both locomotives were 1920s Baldwins, a comparison shows how different two designs of the same wheel arrangement could be. In the mountainous terrain of eastern Cuba, a track crew paused in their labors while 1914 Baldwin Consolidation No. 1391 (below) brought loaded cars to the Central Rafael Freyre mill in 1990.

Left, John B. Charles   Two upper photos, Ron Ziel   Below, Nils Huxtable

The 4-6-0 type was a versatile dual-service locomotive; its two-axle pilot truck allowing for high speeds and the absence of a trailing axle placing more weight on the driving wheels, thus increasing tractive effort. The Ten-wheeler was not common on the Cuban sugar mill railways; however, those that did survive into the late 20th Century were among the most handsome on the island. 1916 Alco-built No. 1749 (opposite), shuffling through palm trees at Central Argentina, near the town of Florida, was a typical engine of the World War I era. No. 1504 (above), a 1923 Baldwin graduate, was smoking up the yard at Central Eduardo García Lavandero, near Artemisa, on March 22, 1981. Another Alco 4-6-0, built in 1916, Central Venezuela No. 1657 (below) was backing a cut of cars to the mill near Ciego de Ávila. Still active at nearly eighty years of age, No. 1657 was considered by many to be the best-proportioned of all Cuban locomotives.

Three photos, Ron Ziel

While the Cuban sugar mills abounded in antiquated steam locos and fascinating operations, the scenery was often less than spectacular: endless fields of sugar cane or cluttered and often cramped *central* yards. One of the more notable exceptions was the lush, hilly vistas of Central Rafael Freyre, where 1912 Baldwin 2-8-0 No. 1390 (upper left) was bringing a train of empties out of the fields, and No. 1391 (above), a locomotive identical but two years newer, was moving loaded cars in 1990. More typical of the level cane country was the car loader on the Central Mal Tiempo, near Cruces, where shining No. 1238 (below), built by Baldwin in 1925, assembled her train; the foreman's horse was tethered in the foreground.

Below, Ron Ziel

Two upper photos, Nils Huxtable

Opposite, Ron Ziel   Above, John B. Charles   Below, Wayne Weiss

While Baldwin was producing locomotives for Cuba in pro-
digious quantities – especially 2-8-0s – in the early 1920s, the
American Locomotive Company was also supplying the needs
of the sugar industry, often with engines more modern and
better-looking. Most Baldwins were arriving with 19th Century
technology slide valve cylinders, while the majority of Alcos
had piston valves. The hog rooting around the Marcelo Salado
mill yard ignored Consolidation No. 1549 (opposite, top) as the
shining 1920 Alco brought in a trainload of cane at sunset.
Larger 2-8-0 No. 1818 (opposite, bottom) was erected by Alco
just four months later. Assigned to Central 10 de Octubre in
1981 when she was working the mill near Ranchuelo, the engine had had the connecting rods to the rear driving wheels
removed, transforming the 2-8-0 into a very slippery 2-6-2!
Despite anti-American feelings promoted by the Castro regime,
two mills retained the names of universally respected *Yanqui*
presidents, George Washington and Abraham Lincoln (the former
a revolutionary, the latter a social democrat?). In 1990, Mogul
No. 1556 (above), a 1920 Baldwin graduate, spewed black oil
smoke over the Central George Washington cane fields in low
sunlight, her old Pyle National headlight having been modified
with a sealed-beam automobile lamp, as was done with many of
the mill engines. A common sight in cane fields around the
world, stalks litter the right-of-way, owing to the practice of
heaping the loads as high as possible in the transporting ve-
hicles, be they ox carts, railroad cars, tractor wagons or trucks.
The largest and the newest Cuban sugar *central* steam locomotive was 2-8-2 No. 1850 (right), built by Baldwin in 1935. After
being stored out of service for years, the Mikado was assigned
to Central Efraín Alfonso in 1990, where she is seen bringing in
a train of cane on March 21, 1994.

251

The standard-gauge Moguls could raise a smoky tempest when the crews decided to thrash them a bit, as was the case with Central Carlos Caraballo No. 1550 (opposite), as she was returning to the engine terminal near Ranchuelo after a long day's work. Central Rafael Reyes No. 1581 (right, above) strained to haul a capacity train through the *Ferrocarril de Cuba* yard in San Luis. Central Venezuela was one of the most active of the sugar lines, with eight serviceable locomotives, three of which worked the mill yard during the peak harvest season. Well-groomed twin 1920 Baldwins 2-8-0s Nos. 1742 and 1743 (bottom) chugged about their shunting chores, with stablemate 4-6-0 No. 1657 in the background.

Three photos, Ron Ziel

Another trim Central Rafael Reyes 2-6-0 at San Luis was Baldwin No. 1452 (above), in the terminal on March 25, 1981. Central 14 de Julio, which maintained a vast 30-inch gauge system in the cane fields near Abreus, had a fleet of well-maintained outside-frame Baldwin 2-8-0s. Once No. 1332 (background smoke) had cleared the yard approach, sister No. 1345 (below) accelerated on the last lap of her run from the distant cane loaders to the mill. Erupting black smoke under puffy white cloud formations, Central Efraín Alfonso No. 1635 (right),

a Baldwin 2-6-2 of 1925 vintage, powered a cane train past a field still to be harvested. What was to be perhaps the final chapter in the saga of Cuban steam-power began in 1994, when ten German 52-class 2-10-0s were reportedly on their way from Poland to alleviate the *Ferrocarril de Cuba* mainline motive-power shortage. The Decapods would be the biggest steam engines to operate in the country. Politics aside, Cuba was a land where steam railroading seemed even sweeter than in other countries beneath the red star.

Two photos, Ron Ziel

Right, Nils Huxtable

After being interrogated and released by the local *Milicija* at Spebrnik, Bosnia, and warned not to photograph any more trains, the author got this ex-German *Kriegslok* as he drove out of town in November, 1970.   Ron Ziel

FURTHER READING

Authors' note: Only English titles are listed. There are many publications in other languages. This listing makes no claim to be completely definitive; it is just a guide to the more widely-circulated materials.

BOOKS

A HISTORY OF RUSSIAN RAILWAYS. J. N. Westwood
George Allen and Unwin Ltd., London. 1964

SOVIET RAILWAYS TODAY. J. N. Westwood
Ian Allan Ltd., London. 1964

RUSSIAN STEAM LOCOMOTIVES. H. M. LeFleming
and J. H. Price; Drake Publishers, Inc., New York. 1972

THE STEAM LOCOMOTIVES OF EASTERN EUROPE.
A. E. Durrant; Newton Abbot, Devon. 1966

THE LAST STEAM LOCOMOTIVES OF EASTERN
EUROPE. P. Ransome-Wallis; Ian Allan Ltd.,
London. 1974

HUNGARIAN RAILROADS. P. M. Kalla-Bishop
Drake Publishers Inc., New York. 1973

STEAM LOCOMOTIVES OF YUGOSLAVIA. Tadej Braté
Wien. 1971

LOCOMOTIVES IN CHINA. Peter Clark
Newcastle, NSW. 1983

THE TWILIGHT OF WORLD STEAM. Ron Ziel and
Mike Eagleson; Grosset & Dunlap, New York. 1973

STEEL RAILS TO VICTORY. Ron Ziel
Hawthorn Books Inc., New York. 1970

MAGAZINE ARTICLES

STEAM IN SIBERIA! Ron Ziel TRAINS, July, 1971

SOVIET STEAM IN SEVENTY-FIVE. Nils Huxtable
RAILWAY MAGAZINE, Sep., 1975

LOCO LIBRARY - P36 4-8-4.
THE WORLD OF TRAINS, Part 94

SPYING ON STEAM. Nils Huxtable
RAILWAY MAGAZINE, May, 1977

VILNIUS REVISITED - A POSTSCRIPT. Nils Huxtable
RAILWAY MAGAZINE, Apr., 1976

HOW GOOD ARE THE RUSSIANS AT RAILROADING?
J.N. Westwood; TRAINS, Aug., 1958

THE TRUMAN LOCOMOTIVES OF POLAND. Ron Ziel
RAIL CLASSICS, July, 1975

MIKADOS IN THE SNOW (Poland). Nils Huxtable
RAILWAY MAGAZINE, Feb., 1982

STEAM IN POLAND. Joel Spencer Rice
RAIL CLASSICS, Sep., 1981

GOODBYE TO THE P-8s (Poland). Nils Huxtable
RAILWAY MAGAZINE, June, 1980

ON BORROWED STEAM (Rumania). Ron Ziel
RAIL CLASSICS, May, 1976

STEAM IN POLAND TODAY. Steve Brown
RAILFAN, April, 1993

TRIALS AND TRIBULATIONS (East Europe). Ron Ziel
TRAINS, Aug., 1977

RED STAR STEAM (Czechoslovakia). Nils Huxtable
RAIL CLASSICS, May, 1980

EAST GERMANY'S DISTINCTIVE STEAMERS. Ron Ziel
RAIL CLASSICS, Nov., 1978

CHAIRMAN MAO'S RAILROADS. Don Phillips
TRAINS, Nov., 1972

RAILFANNING: CHINA STYLE. Greg Nazarow
RAILFAN, Dec., 1990

CHINA: BIG STEAM'S LAST STAND. Lloyd D. Lewis
TRAINS, March, 1992

SUGARLAND EXPRESS (Cuba). Nils Huxtable
LOCOMOTIVE & RAILWAY PRESERVATION,
July-Aug., 1990

VIDEOS

Movies of steam in action during the Communist era are virtually non-existent. GOODHEART PRODUCTIONS, P.O. Box 47131-Z, Chicago, Illinois 60647 USA, produces excellent VHS and Beta videos of the great steam specials on former red star railways.

   Printed in USA by Walsworth Publishing

While *Deutsche Reichsbahn* 4-6-2 No. 01 2118 wheeled an Intraflug Pullman special out of the yard at Saalfeld, East Germany on May 28, 1981, semi-streamlined Pacific No. 01 0513 left the station with a regular train to Camburg. This was typical of the dramatic action that could be seen daily in the era of *Steam Beneath the Red Star*.   - Pete Skelton